Microeconomics

Dave Blight & Tony Shafto

Senior Lecturers in Industrial Economics
Coventry Polytechnic.

Hutchinson

London Sydney Auckland Johannesburg

Hutchinson Education

An imprint of Century Hutchinson Ltd
62–65 Chandos Place, London WC2N 4NW

Century Hutchinson Australia Pty Ltd
89–91 Albion Street, Surry Hills,
New South Wales 2010, Australia

Century Hutchinson New Zealand Ltd
PO Box 40–086, Glenfield, Auckland 10,
New Zealand

Century Hutchinson South Africa (Pty) Ltd
PO Box 337, Bergvlei, 2012 South Africa

This edition first published 1989

Set in Times Med rom
by Hope Services
Printed and bound in Great Britain by
Anchor Press Ltd, Tiptree, Essex

British Library Cataloguing in Publication Data

Shafto, T.A.C. (Thomas Anthony Cheshire)
Microeconomics
I. Title II. Blight, Dave
338.5

ISBN 0–09–175685–5

Contents

Preface

The Introduction to Microeconomics computer discs and student text grew out of our combined teaching experience and desire to make wide use of the microcomputer. Experience has shown us that students too often emerge from courses in foundation level economics with the most muddled ideas about costs, revenues and market structures and the rather naive belief that the theory of market economics bears little relation to the 'real' world of business.

Our aim has been to provide a thorough examination of the basic concepts, relationships and analytical techniques of microeconomics and to indicate how these relate to practical business problems and decisions. We believe that today, when the respective roles of the private and public sectors of the economy are under intensive scrutiny, it is more than ever necessary to ensure that the basic principles of the market economy are clearly understood. This understanding, combined with the ability to handle basic analytical techniques, is also an essential foundation for more advanced studies in business and industrial economics.

For the most part the material included is the generally accepted core of modern microeconomics, but we have extended this to provide a brief analysis of the consumer welfare implications of market structures, an introduction to investment appraisal linked to the computer disc program, and an introduction to demand estimation and the use of regression analysis, again linked to the disc program.

The order in which the material is developed is slightly different from that normally adopted. We have introduced production theory and isoquant/isocost analysis rather earlier than most books, because we believe that a thorough study of costs is basic to an understanding of economics. Moreover our experience suggests that students find isoquant/isocost analysis far easier to grasp than the abstract concepts of consumer theory and indifference curves.

The student text deliberately contains very little institutional or applied material because major policy reviews are being undertaken by government in the areas of industrial/anti-trust policy, industrial relations and public sector control, and anything written now is likely to become quickly outdated. Up-to-date information in these areas can be found in the *British Economy Survey*, the *Economist* and in *An Introduction to the UK Economy* by Harbury and Lipsey (Pitman 1983).

At the end of each chapter are a few essay questions to test understanding of the concepts developed in the chapter. However, the main vehicles for testing understanding are the two computer discs, which contain three types of teaching material. These are:

1 Eight sections of self-assessment questions which closely follow the chapters of the book. In these the student's knowledge of the concepts is carefully examined in a logical order. Wrong answers to any question are immediately signalled, and a brief explanation of the relevant points is provided. At the end of the section a mark is given, together with remedial advice concerning the chapters to be revised. Student answers can be recorded on disc for later scrutiny by the teacher.
2 Six simulations which allow the student to use the basic economic principles in 'practical' situations.
3 Two calculation programs designed to take the drudgery out of investment appraisal and regresssion analysis, in order to bring these two useful and practical techniques within the scope of normal classroom teaching. Users of the regression program are referred to the Central Statistical Office's **Guide to Official Statistics** as an invaluable guide to economic statistics

While preparing the discs and textbook we received valuable help, constructive criticism and advice from our colleagues at the Coventry (Lanchester) Polytechnic. In particular, we wish to express our gratitude to Martin Webster, whose programming skills averted disaster and despair on numerous occasions. We would also like to thank John Proops of the University of Keele for allowing us to include his simulation 'USSR'; the Economics Association for affording us facilities to introduce the discs to members at the 1983 Loughborough conference; many other teachers for allowing us to invade their classrooms and to test our material on their students; and, of course, the Coventry (Lanchester) Polytechnic for the use of some excellent equipment and facilities. Finally, we wish to thank our wives for their patience and understanding; sometimes, we fear, under great provocation.

Dave Blight & Tony Shafto
1983

Preface to the new edition

Since this book was first published it has been used as a text for a wide range of courses both with and without the computer software package of the same title, now published by Tutor software, Wishaw, Sutton Coldfield. This new edition has been revised and extended to include a fuller discussion of competition and public policy. There is a completely new chapter (10) on rivalry in imperfect markets, including oligopolistic behaviour and price discrimination. This extension will make the book even more attractive to first year courses, especially those for business and business related studies.

David Blight & Tony Shafto
1988

1

The economic problem

Economic Activity

The fundamental concern of economics is with production to satisfy human wants using the resources available. This apparently simple statement contains many important implications. We have to recognise that the wants of individuals and communities are varied and probably limitless, whereas the world's resources are finite and the knowledge of how to make use of available resources is limited.

Economics cannot claim to solve the basic imbalance of production and desire, but it can provide a set of concepts, techniques and analytical skills which can clarify problems and shed light on a wide range of practical issues of concern to the modern world. Given the limitation of resources, it can help to clarify fundamental decisions that have to be made regarding **what and how much should be produced and for whose benefit** the priorities of production should be arranged. In developing the skills which the economist can offer to his fellows, the microcomputer is showing itself to be an invaluable tool. It takes away the drudgery, errors and fears which, in the past, have been barriers to those applying 'manual' methods of calculation to relationships capable of expression in mathematical language. We can now have on our desks models and simulations that are a great deal closer to the reality we seek to understand than anything that can be produced on paper. Calculating has become simple, accurate and swift, so that it has become more important than ever that we should have a clear understanding of the concepts and relationships that we wish to examine.

To return, then, to the opening statement, we need to define rather more precisely the main terms that it contains.

Wants

Some writers refer to needs. We prefer the expression **wants** because we wish to stress that an economic want does not imply a biological need. A want exists if people are prepared to sacrifice some of their resources in order to satisfy it. It need not be necessary to their survival nor even beneficial. It may even be harmful or dangerous. The economist, as such, expresses neither moral nor medical judgements on wants, nor does he attempt to rank them in order of value. If people are prepared to give up their resources to obtain tobacco or heroin, go hang-gliding and play space invaders, then all these are wants that can be measured and analysed.

We do, however, classify wants and the goods and services produced to satisfy them in various ways. One useful way is to distinguish between:

1 **Personal wants,** seen as the satisfaction of individual or family desires for items such as private cars, computer games, foreign holidays or houses to live in; and
2 **Community wants,** seen as the satisfaction of the desire of the community to advance the general well-being of the group, through benefits such as public sanitation, paved roads, street lights, fire protection and the prevention of violent crime, infectious diseases and so on.

Goods and services produced to satisfy personal wants may be termed **private goods**. Those produced to satisfy community wants may be termed **public goods**. Some care is needed in identifying public goods. For instance, some goods or services such as sports centres and municipal golf courses, provided by local authorities for public use are not really public goods. They are available for individuals to use if they so wish. Those who do not, gain no benefit from them. Contrast this position with the genuine public good provided by, say, a sewerage system which helps to prevent the outbreak of infectious diseases. The whole community benefits from the eradication and control of diseases such as cholera and diptheria.

Resources

The basic resource necessary for production to take place will always remain human effort, both physical and mental. In addition, people have learned to use many of the resources of nature such as metals, swiftly flowing water, the fertility of the land and others. They have also learned to make tools, some of which, like the wheel, the steam engine, the electric motor and the computer, have had revolutionary consequences for people's patterns of living. These resources, known as factors of production and consisting of labour, land and capital, are analysed more carefully later.

Production

The widest economic definition of production includes any part of total activity or chain of interrelated activities involved in the satisfaction of personal or community wants. This, therefore, includes not only the manufacture of goods, such as television sets, or the actual provision of services, such as hairdressing or sports instruction, but also those activities necessary to identify wants and to ensure that goods and services created do actually reach the people wanting them. Production, in this wide sense, includes marketing and finance, research and exploration, the distribution of goods and the work of organisations such as the police and licensing authorities that regulate and maintain order and so make other daily activities possible. Notice that production involves the transformation of the basic resources of nature and human energy into some form of physical object or activity that satisfies individual or community wants.

Almost all forms of production do require some use of resources and some expenditure of human effort. Any benefit or satisfaction of a want that is achieved without this expenditure is termed a **free good**. Rain falling on a garden is a free good in this sense but rainwater collected in a reservoir and pumped through pipes has used resources and is no longer free but is a normal **economic good**. Similarly, the air we breathe on a country walk is free but air pumped into a mine or the air in the pressurised cabin of an airliner has required resources and is an economic good.

As economists, we should be careful not to suggest that any productive activity is somehow superior to any other. The economist can indicate whether certain forms of production are likely to achieve certain stated objectives. He can calculate the implications of using resources in one way rather than in another. He must leave it to the political institutions of the community, within which, of course, he may play his own individual part, to decide what the objectives are and what choices must be made. It is essentially a political decision, for example, whether resources are used to provide defence against possible hostile countries, or to provide schoolchildren with meals or textbooks or computers.

Choice and Scarcity

Production, then, offers a variety of possibilities. If you have a spare evening, you can use it to go to a cinema with a friend, to play badminton, to watch television or to study economics. You must choose between these competing possibilities because you cannot do them all at the same time. Similarly, if there is an empty plot of land in a town centre, the local authority for that town may use it for a car park, an office block, a factory, a school, a block of private flats or for any other use they can devise. Some might want it to be left empty as a reserve for wild flowers. What is certain is that the plot of land cannot be used for all these purposes together at the same time. Resources of all kinds are scarce in relation to wants which, appear to be insatiable because, when any resources are used for activity A they are being denied to activities B, C, D and so on. If the resources are to be used at all, then choices have to be made. Economics is constantly involved in the identification and measurement of choices in the use of resources of competing ends.

Production Possibilities

Production requires the contribution of production factors. In any community a given supply of production factors has to be used to provide the range of goods and services required by that community. We have already recognised that factors used to produce A cannot, at the same time, be used to produce B. Choices have to be made.

This idea can be further illustrated if we simplify the problem and think in terms of two competing products or groups of products only; say, food and durables. The following table shows the possible production of various combinations of food and durables open to a community with its existing stock of resources or factors of production and with its existing level of technical knowledge:

Food	*Durables*
1000	0
800	500
600	950
400	1180
200	1275
0	1320

This table is the basis for the **production possibility curve** of Fig. 1.1. This curve represents the production boundary of the community which can

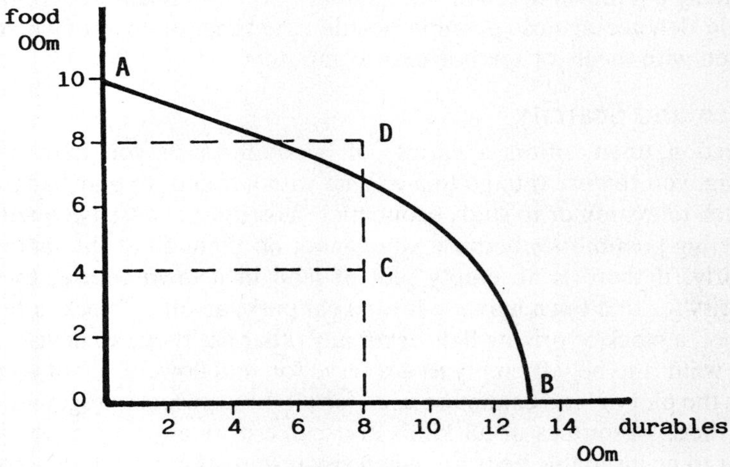

Fig. 1.1 The production possibilities curve
The community can produce any combination of food and durables along or within, but not outside the production possibilities curve **AB**.

produce any combination of food and durables on or within the curve. If it produces within the curve, say, at C (400 million units of food and 800 million units of durables) it will not be using all its resources. Some will be unemployed. On the other hand, it cannot reach the combination D (800 million units each, of food and durables) because this is beyond the curve and so beyond the production capabilities of the community with its present stock of resources and present level of technology. If the community wishes to push total production beyond the curve it must gain more factors and/or develop new skills and knowledge of how to combine the factors to produce a greater volume of production.

Notice the shape of the curve and the changes that it depicts. When production of food falls from the high level of 1000 million units to 800 million, the lost 200 million units are replaced by 500 million units of durables. However, when the next 200 million units of food are sacrificed, the gain in durables is only 450 million units. Looking at this another way and starting from the zero (0) level of food production, each 200 million units of food that is gained costs progressively more durables.

The implication here is that it is possible to transfer production factors from one form of production to another but not with equal results. The shape of the curve suggests that the first resources to be transferred from, say food to durables, are the ones least suitable for food and most suitable for durables production. However, as more are transferred the reverse becomes more likely. The costs of transfer are increasing. We can say, in fact, that the basic assumption underlying this curve is that of **increasing opportunity costs**. The term 'opportunity cost' is explained in the next section. There are some questions relating to the curve in section 1 of the computer questions and the computer games WELLAND and USSR are on the theme of choice between competing claims for scarce resources.

Cost

When a choice is made and resources are employed for one particular activity then, as we have already seen, that activity has a cost. This takes two forms, absolute and opportunity cost.

Absolute Cost

We can measure the absolute cost in terms of the quantity of resources used. For example, you can say that you spent two hours of your time in playing badminton. Similarly, the local authority can say that it devoted half a hectare of land to the provision of a sports centre.

Opportunity Cost

Another possibility is to measure the cost in terms of the next best or the next preferred alternative choice to the one actually adopted. For example, you could say that the game of badminton has cost the chance of watching a particular television programme. The opposition party in the local authority could argue that the cost of the sports centre was a block of flats that it would have built had it been in power. This cost, measured in terms of the sacrificed alternative, is called the **opportunity cost**.

Notice that it can be difficult, and sometimes controversial, to attempt to measure the opportunity cost. Your friend, for example, might see the cost of your game of badminton as the visit to the cinema which did not materialise. A third party in the local authority might have seen the cost of the sports centre as a factory. Nevertheless, opportunity cost is an extremely important concept. It lies behind almost all central and local government decisions concerning the use of resources. It is the cost that must always concern the business manager when he decides to take one course of action rather than another and when he commits his available resources to one particular line of production.

Notice that we have not mentioned money in either of these definitions of cost. This is because money is not itself a resource. It is, however, a useful measuring device and a medium or aid to exchange. It often helps us to compare costs. Using money values may aid the comparison of one set of resources with another, or one benefit with another. Neverthless the use of money, useful as it is, must not blind us to the true nature of the costs involved.

Making Choices

If economic decisions frequently involve choosing between alternative uses for scarce resources it follows that there has to be some mechanism for making these choices. Economists are interested in the decision making mechanism, not so much because of the processes involved as because the nature of the mechanism is likely to influence the objectives or benefits sought and the options actually chosen. A political party which has dominated a local authority for a long time is likely to use spare land in a different way from one which is in danger of losing power at the next election. Your choice of whether to play badminton, go to the cinema, watch television or study may depend on whether or not your friend or anyone other than yourself has a share in making the decision.

For simplicity, we usually identify two broad ways of making economic decisions. These are by political process or by individual choice.

Political Process

When the mechanism is controlled by the political process, the institutions of government or their agents either own or control the factors of production and have powers to direct how they should be employed. Whoever controls the political institutions also controls the economy. If the institutions are sensitive to public opinion and pressure then the economic decisions will be equally sensitive. If they operate by the exercise of absolute power then the economic decisions are more likely to reflect the priorities and objectives of the ruling group with less reference to the wishes of groups lacking political force.

Nevertheless, the decision makers are still faced with the need to make choices. They cannot escape from the basic economic facts of scarce resources and unlimited wants. The German National Socialist Party recognised this fact when, in the 1930s, it offered the German nation the choice between 'guns or butter'. The choice that was made was to have consequences far beyond the economy of Germany. A different political system might have made a different choice.

If a political system does take over the task of making economic decisions it will need machinery to gather information concerning the resources available, the possible uses of those resources and some means of measuring costs and benefits. It will have to make decisions and put them into effect. It may find that a considerable quantity of resources have to be employed just to operate the decision-making machinery before any further production is achieved.

In spite of the difficulties, most societies reserve at least some of the major resource decisions to their political machinery.

Individual Choice

Individual choice operates through what may be called the forces of supply and demand interacting in a market. These terms are examined more closely in later sections. At this stage we simply need to recognise that a market system of choice implies that total demand is made up of the combined decisions of large numbers of buyers. The purchase of final goods and services, those satisfying community or individual needs, is called **consumption**. The decision making unit of consumption is often taken to be the household, but to avoid having to distinguish between households and their members we can use the general term **consumer**. It is consumers who decide what to buy – and what not to buy.

In the same way, total supply is made up of the combined decisions of production units which, for simplicity, we can call firms, concerning what to supply or what not to supply. These decisions are made by the firms' owners and managers.

These forces of consumption and production, which we can also see in terms of demand for and supply of goods and services, interact through the prices buyers are willing to pay and suppliers willing to accept. Price represents the value of resources which buyers are willing and able to sacrifice to obtain the desired product. It also represents the payment which suppliers receive in exchange for the products they offer. Price is normally expressed in terms of money but it can take other forms – for example, the 'A' level examination grades which aspiring university candidates have to 'pay' to obtain the places they desire.

Economic Systems

An economic system refers to the way in which resources necessary for production are controlled and allocated and consequently to the pattern of production which results, i.e. the mixture of goods and services that are produced. It also concerns the methods of production – how they are produced – and the pattern of distribution – who receives what is produced. These are the questions, referred to earlier, of What?, How much? and For whom?

There are several ways of classifying economic systems. One way is to classify according to:

a **Ownership of resources** and who controls the means of production and distribution; and
b **The distribution of production** whether distribution takes place through political processes or through the mechanism of the market.

Resources may be owned and controlled by the political institutions of the State, by private individuals or by collections of individuals acting together in the pursuit of common interests.

Distribution, as we have already seen, can be controlled by political institutions or by a market guided by prices. Systems which favour the political control of resources also tend to favour the political control of distribution, but there can be exceptions. The British National Health System is politically controlled and services are distributed on the basis of need rather than on the ability or willingness to pay a money price. Its ordinary day-to-day medical services, however, are provided by independent groups of general practitioner doctors. On the other hand, in 1988 electricity supply organisations were State-owned but electricity was distributed through a price mechanism. Coal was mined by the State-owned British Coal and distributed to private households through a price system. Indeed, the State has used prices to influence demand for fuel, for example, by raising the price of gas in the early 1980s to reduce demand and the pressure to employ resources in gas production.

The Price System

When we refer to a price system, also called a market, or unregulated market economy, we are implying that decisions of buyers are influenced by the prices of products on sale in the various product markets. The individual buyer is not concerned with how these prices are determined – whether, for example, they are fixed by a powerful supplier or arrived at through the interaction of the total market forces of supply and demand. The individual can do nothing on his own to alter the prices but his decision regarding what to buy, how much to buy and what combination of products to buy will be influenced by price. To the individual, the price represents the sacrifice he has to make to obtain the desired product and he can relate this to benefit he gains from it. Accordingly, he can decide whether the benefit is worth the sacrifice.

Although we are not usually conscious of this process this is what we really imply when we make comments such as 'That dress is not worth £100' or 'I am not paying that fare to go by train when I can go by coach for half the cost'.

At this stage we can make certain general assumptions about the operation of a price system. Some of these are examined more closely later. We assume that:

1 More will be bought at a lower price than at a higher price so that raising the price of a product, other conditions remaining the same, will reduce the quantity of that product that people want to buy.
2 When there are two or more products offering benefits considered to be of equal value, people will refer the product whose price is the lowest. Notice that we are referring to value as perceived by possible buyers. We are not making any assumptions about the physical properties of alternative products. A and B may have almost identical physical properties but if A is perceived by the buyer as being superior to B, perhaps because of the reputation of the producer, then willingness to pay a higher price for A is taken as evidence that A offers the greater benefit. The economist, as an economist, does not pass judgement on the preference, but simply observes and records. Similarly, he does not pass judgement on decisions arrived at through the political mechanism.

The Planned Economy

At the other extreme to the price or unregulated market system there is the fully regulated or planned economy. Here, all choice decisions are made by the political machinery of the State, which is also likely to own or control the economic resources of the community. The State then has to estimate the costs and benefits of the various choices open to it and make decisions in accordance with its political, social and economic objectives.

The Mixed Economy

In practice, most economic systems contain a mixture of State planning and unregulated markets – even if the markets are not always officially recognized by the political rulers. When, however, there is a substantial and openly recognised mixture of State planning and market/price distribution the term **mixed economy** is usually used. The economies of the Western European countries are often quoted as examples of balanced mixed economies. The degree to which State planning and free or unregulated market distribution are mixed can vary considerably from one country to another. This is clearly a fruitful field for political controversy and it is often difficult to separate the economic from the political and social issues. If the economist has a specialist contribution to make to this debate it is to attempt to compare the costs and benefits associated with the different systems of resource ownership and decision making.

Comparison of Systems

If we comment on the 'efficiency' of one economic system as compared with another, we have to be careful to avoid introducing our own valuations or **value judgements** – the term normally given to opinions expressed or implied concerning relative values. We have to judge the successes and failures of any system by its own standards and objectives. If the objective of a system appears to be to provide a wide range of consumer goods to the largest possible number of people then this is the yardstick by which success must be measured. We cannot say that the system has failed if it is unable to prevent the invasion of a friendly country by an aggressive neighbour. On the other hand, if the object claimed is to strengthen national defences then we would expect it to be able to defend the allied country, if necessary, at the cost of providing fewer motorcars or less candy floss for its own consumers.

It is difficult, then, for the economist to compare the efficiency or degree of success of different systems, if their objectives are different. What we do have to recognise, however, are signs that systems are failing to achieve their declared or implied objectives. We should also recognise indications that the objectives are not compatible with possible achievement, taking into account the resources available.

When we compare the problems that emerge in each of the systems of State and free market distribution, we find that these are often very similar, although the symptoms can be rather different. Most problems tend to fall into one of the following categories:

1 The pattern of wants is different from that of production, giving rise to a surplus of some goods and services and a shortage of others.
2 People are trying to obtain more goods and services than can be produced from available resources.
3 Existing resources do not meet the needs of a changing production system so that some sources seeking employment are unable to find it.

This problem, which we recognise as **unemployment** may be more evident in a market system based on individual choice than in one controlled by political institutions because in the latter it may be possible to direct resources, including labour, to activities considered necessary. When, of course, we start to consider the implications of directing labour we find ourselves facing issues beyond the scope of this book.

In a price system free from outside regulation it can be claimed that supply usually equals demand because the price moves in order to bring the two into equilibrium. What cannot be guaranteed is that this equilibrium will always be at quantity and price levels that are acceptable to society and in accordance with current views of what is morally just. When this consideration enters the calculation then society has to decide how much regulation it is prepared to accept in order to achieve the result it desires. It must also make sure that measures taken by the regulating body do actually achieve the desired objective. The economist may be able to contribute his knowledge of markets and of the decision-making processes among consumers and producers in order to assist this process. We shall see later that policies developed to achieve socially desirable aims, such as ensuring that people are adequately housed, are not always successful.

On the other hand, a price system cannot guarantee that imbalances between desired consumption and actual production will never arise. Food production is notoriously unpredictable and this is another problem which we examine later in both the book and the computer disc questions.

There are no easy answers nor magic wands to ensure that supply and demand are always at an ideal level. The economist cannot offer Utopia but he can offer an understanding of the forces at work and can hope to guide policymakers and others who are involved in making the difficult decisions of how to satisfy the many conflicting wants of the community from available scarce resources.

Exercises Relating to Chapter 1

1 A leading economist once suggested that the economic attitudes of his country produced 'private affluence and public squalor'. What do you think he meant? What are the possible consequences of 'public squalor' and what choices have to be made to avoid them?

2 Discuss, with examples, the problems likely to arise when trying to compare the economic performance of two countries which are politically, socially and culturally different.

3 Below is a simplified summary of the income and expenditure of a local borough council in 1983/4. Suppose the council wished to increase its spending on refuse collection. What options are open to it? Explain the economic concepts involved.

Income (£ million)		*Expenditure (£ million)*	
House rents and charges	4.7	Housing maintenance and services	9.7
Government grants and subsidies	6.7	Recreation, parks, sports, cultural and burial services	3.9
General fees and charges	3.6	Health, refuse collection, street cleaning and environmental control	1.7
Rates (local taxes)	3.6	Planning, development, car parks and other services	3.3
Total	18.6		18.6

2

Production

Nature of Production

In Chapter 1, production was explained in terms of the satisfaction of wants through the provision of goods or services, a process called the **creation of utility**. This general term avoids any problems of explaining how or what sort of satisfaction is gained. For example, if Mr Jones buys a motor car he may do so because he wants a means of transport to travel to work, or because he wants to impress the neighbours, or because he wants to enjoy a motoring holiday in Europe. All these different forms of satisfaction can be grouped under the general term **utility**.

Factors of Production

Production is achieved by the use of one or more **factors of production**. These were identified in Chapter 1 as labour, land and capital.

Labour
For convenience, **labour** is usually denoted by the symbol **L**. Labour is really the basic or fundamental factor because nothing makes itself. There has to be some human agency at work and this, whether physical or mental activity is what we mean by the factor labour.

Capital
Capital is a general term used to describe man-made aids to production. These are necessary for even the simplest forms of manufacture or service. The hairdresser requires at least a pair of scissors; the entertainer in a local club has a stage and a microphone. These aids to production, the equipment, machines, vehicles and buildings which assist people to product utility are all included in **capital**, which is usually denoted by the symbol **K**. This is not because economists cannot spell, but because **C** is usually reserved for consumption, the process of making use of production.

Notice that we have used the term capital to mean actual physical goods. To avoid confusion we can stress this by using terms such as **physical capital, real capital or capital assets**. Possibilities for confusion arise because people frequently refer to capital when they mean the finance used to acquire physical assets. This can, for clarity, be described as **money or financial capital**.

In practice, we do not always distinguish very carefully between the two because it is often convenient to refer to capital in general terms, rather than to specific items of equipment or of money. As long as we remember what is implied then this does not usually matter when we are simply concerned with the general analysis of production and the employment of production factors.

Natural resources and land

The general term **land** is often used with a double meaning to include both the space required for production activities, the sites for factories, shops, etc, and the resources of nature which can be used in production and which may be extracted from land, sea and air.

It is preferable to keep these senses distinct because land as an area of location has rather different characteristics from those of natural resources such as metal ores, wood and chemicals. Accordingly, the separate symbols, **S** for site location and **R** for resources, are often employed.

Enterprise

Many textbooks offer enterprise as the final, essential factor. The owner of a business enterprise is regarded as the mainspring of production, as the **entrepreneur** who supplies the initiative, takes the risks and receives the rewards of production. However, there are some difficulties with this approach. In the first place, we cannot be quite sure what we mean by **enterprise**. Since a very high proportion of all new business ventures fail in the first year of life, much enterprise might be better termed foolhardiness or wishful thinking. As we shall see in this chapter, we normally expect there to be a clear and calculable relationship between the amount of a factor fed into a business – the amount of factor input – and the amount of production achieved – the volume of output. There is no certainty that this relationship holds with enterprise or risktaking. Certainly there are unavoidable risks in business but successful business management might be seen as reducing or avoiding, rather than increasing these. Altogether the idea of treating enterprise as an entirely separate factor of production creates too many problems and we do not include it in the computer calculations relating to this area of analysis.

Rewards of Production Factors

The owners of factors of production expect payment in return for allowing them to be used in production. Each factor, therefore, has an appropriate reward. This, as we see later, can be regarded as a factor price. At this stage we simply identify the rewards.

Wages

Wage is here used as a general term denoting the reward or return to the factor, labour. It includes all forms of salary, bonus, commission or other similar payments.

Interest

Interest is the price of using capital. Interest cannot be ignored even if capital is supplied by, or accumulated from the earnings of the business. If it were not used in the enterprise, capital could be hired to others outside the organisation in return for interest. Remember the basic economic concept of **opportunity cost**. A firm which uses its own accumulated capital ought not to overlook interest foregone, the opportunity cost of using the capital.

Rent

Rent is the general term applied to the price paid for the use of land. As with the use of capital, the business firm using land owned by itself and for which it pays no actual rent, ought to remember the opportunity cost. Space can be hired to others and so, usually, has a price. Owners of natural resources normally receive payments for the right to extract them. Such payments may be looked on as a form of rent, although often they are termed **royalties**.

Profit

Profit is strictly a 'residual' from the earnings of a business. It is the revenue remaining after all the factor costs of land, resources, labour and capital have been met. Traditionally, it was assumed that this residual was the reward earned by successful enterprise. However, we have already noted the problem of treating enterprise as a distinct production factor. In addition, we have the further difficulty that the profit earned by a limited company belongs legally to the company's ordinary shareholders and, in the case of large companies, these shareholders play no actual part in managing or directing the business. Further aspects of profit and the way it is defined and used by a number of leading economists are discussed in the Appendix to Chapter 8.

Profit, then, can scarcely be seen as a reward for successful enterprise and the taking of business risks. The rewards and risks of successful share speculation are rather different. In the case of established companies the risks taken by the original shareholders and founders of the business are also not directly relevant to the issue.

Some, especially Marxist observers, would argue that the residual profit belongs to those who risk their livelihoods by working in the enterprise. They would claim that profit belongs to labour. Clearly, profit is a difficult and important concept and presents problems, some of which are discussed in the Appendix to Chapter 8. At this stage, however, we have to avoid the controversies and recognise it simply as the balance of business earnings after all the factor payments have been made.

Combining Factors

Production can only very rarely be achieved by one factor alone. Normally it requires some combination of factors. A hairdresser, for example, requires somewhere to sit the customer (S), some equipment (K) and his or her own skill and effort (L). A cut-glass factory, one of the few modern organisations in which raw materials enter a factory and finished consumer goods leave, requires a site area (S), the basic or raw materials used in making glass (R), a range of machines (K) and many highly skilled workers (L).

We can, therefore, say that **production**, which we must now start to think of more as **output (Q)**, is the result of combining land (**S**), capital (**K**), and labour (**L**) and sometimes, basic resources (**R**). Combining these factors is the function of the production organisation. It is a small but important step to put this into the language of simple mathematics to say that:

$$Q = f(S,K,L,R)$$

This equation states that output produced (Q) is a function of, or is determined by, quantities of the resources listed inside the brackets. If the quantities or mix of resources change, so will the level of output produced. The precise relationship between resources used and output produced is likely to be different for each good. Consequently, the general symbol 'f' is used in preference to some specific term. It does, however, represent a very special type of function because it always assumes that resources are combined in the most efficient way possible, at the present level of technology. The level of output (Q), is thus the highest possible, given the resources used and the technical knowledge available.

This also suggests that the level of technology is an important influence on the level of output and that technology (T) should be included within the brackets of the equation. Alternatively, we might regard this as something that affects the functional relationship between output and the input of resources. If new processes are developed then an increased level of output can be produced from the same input of raw materials. At this stage, however, the mathematical treatment of technology is not very important, although useful if you wish to understand the calculations underlying some of the computer exercises, especially the production table (Appendix A in the Teacher's Notes) and which is used for some of the questions on short- and long-run costs. Otherwise it is sufficient to be aware of the main elements involved in production.

The Unit of Production

The need to make choices and to combine factors of production before anything can be produced implies that there have to be units for the organisation of production. From time to time we have referred to firms in general terms and we must now examine some aspects of these business organisations more closely.

The Firm in the Private Sector

In the early days of commercial and industrial activity people formed groups to pursue specific trading ventures and when these ended the agreements terminated. As the whole pace of commerce and industry quickened, and as industry developed and became dependent on mills, factories and on increasingly complex and expensive machines, more formal and durable organisational structures became necessary. People could still come together and make their own personal agreements or, with the direct or indirect authority of Parliament, they could form separate business entities called companies or corporations, provided they obeyed rules established by Parliament, or by equivalent organs of government outside the UK. These two distinctions still exist in modern business. We have personal and corporate sectors within that general area of economic activity which is not government owned and controlled and which is known as the **private sector** of the economy.

Personal sector

This term is used in the United Kingdom National Income accounts to describe those business firms which are made up partly of people trading on their own account as sole proprietors or sole traders and for whom there is no really firm division between their personal and their business property. It also consists partly of partnerships which are formed by people who agree to engage in business activities together for common objectives. Although a partnership does usually involve some degree of formal agreement, in the last resort there is still no full legal separation between business and personal property. Partners and sole proprietors are literally risking everything they own when they engage in business. The term 'personal sector' as used here for production organisations should not be confused with its use elsewhere in national accounts to describe ordinary individuals and household consumption.

In times of economic depression the personal sector tends to expand. Between 1979 and 1987 the number of self-employed people in the United Kingdom rose from 1 906 000 to 2 861 000. Although this growth was widespread the main increases were in the service industries, especially banking, finance and insurance, but also in health, recreation, cultural and personal service. In one industry, construction, self-employment expanded although total employment was falling. Some of the larger companies were subcontracting work to smaller firms in preference to taking on more workers themselves. There were some interesting regional differences. In East Anglia, South West England and Wales the self-employed accounted for around 12% of the civilian labour force but in the North the figure was around 7½%

The corporate sector

The disadvantages of the personal forms of business structure are very evident when it comes to accumulating and risking the very large amounts of capital required for modern business. The most common business organisation today is the limited company, or its equivalent in other countries. The company is a legal entity in its own right with an identity separate from its various members. The company's capital is partly provided by shares, holders of which are the legal owners of the company. Shareholders are rewarded by a division of profits called dividend. Further capital is often provided by debentures, which are loans raised and transferred in ways similar to shares. Additional finance may be provided by any other loans that the company can raise through the financial system. Companies are controlled by directors, representing and appointed by the shareholders, and they are run by managers employed under the authority of directors. Companies can be very small. In many, a husband and wife may be the only shareholders, directors and managers. Companies can also be very large. These include the giant multinational enterprises such as General Motors, IBM, ICI, and Unilever. Such organisations control budgets of millions of pounds and employ thousands of workers. If a company declares itself a public company and conforms to the appropriate laws, its shares and debentures can be offered for public sale. The main markets for the sale and transfer of approved shares and debentures are the stock exchanges found in most of the world's financial centres.

There are some business organisations, notably the building societies and the cooperative societies, that do not fit neatly into the two sectors outlined. In spite of their special legal status which is very similar to that of the charities, these organisations are coming increasingly to resemble the large business companies of the corporate sector.

Public Enterprise

The idea that governments should have little or nothing to do with production activities belongs chiefly to the nineteenth century. Earlier governments and ruling systems were often glad of the money-making possibilities of economic enterprise, even if their role might be limited to selling certain monopolies, a **monopoly** being the sole right to manufacture, distribute or import a product.

The twentieth century has seen a considerable extension of government production in the form of providing a wide range of social, educational, health and environmental services and, in many countries, in taking over direct control and ownership of basic industries, such as transport, the provision of fuel and power and some manufacturing industries.

The actual organisational structure of the public sector varies a great deal. The national, central government has a final responsibility in most cases, but may operate through, or in cooperation with, others. These include, for example regional agencies, the British area health authorities, local government bodies and the public corporations set up in the United Kingdom to operate nationalised industries.

Motives for the extension or the contraction of 'public' ownership are often political and ideological but the economist is interested because public sector enterprise disposes of a substantial share of the nation's scarce resources. It is responsible for the satisfaction of needs in such basic areas of activity as education, sanitation, defence, care of the sick, the unfortunate and the old, as well as of the fire, police and other protective services. It is difficult to calculate the precise proportion of national economic activity which is controlled by government but, taking into account the considerable influence of government decisions on industries such as housebuilding, civil engineering, electronics and educational publishing, the proportion is almost certainly over a half and may be as much as two-thirds.

The Production Process

Production Isoquants

We must now consider how output varies when there are changes in the production factors employed. To assist us we can use some very simple techniques of graphical analysis.

You have probably heard of isobars and isotherms. **Iso-** is derived from a Greek word (isos) meaning equal. Economists, regrettably, are sometimes guilty of mixing Greek and Latin roots and an **isoquant** is the term used to denote a line on a graph which joins points of equal total output achievable from varying combinations of production factors. Because a normal graph is two-dimensional we have to illustrate this concept with two factors only and the most convenient and realistic are capital (K) and labour (L). Our production function is thus:

$$Q = f(K,L)$$

The precise shape of the isoquant must depend on the extent to which the factors can be substituted for each other.

Factors with fixed relationships
At one extreme, varying the proportions will not alter the amount that can be produced. This is limited by the capacity of the other factor. For example, if we have a machine which cannot be varied in size or complexity, and which requires one operator, then the possible output level is determined by the number of machines or by the number of operators available.

If we assume that there is no point in having more than one person per machine – or more than one machine per person – then the isoquant is limited to one point only on the graph for each possible level of production. We can draw only a production ray to represent the output increases produced by increasing the quantity of machines and operators employed in the constant proportions dictated by the ruling technical conditions.

This graph shows three rays representing three possible combinations of workers and machines, i.e. labour (L) and capital (K). Consider a production method represented by the ray B. This combines L and K in equal but fixed proportions. One unit of capital and one unit of labour produces 100 units of output (Q) so that K = 1 and L = 1 results in Q = 100. If both K and L are doubled then so too will be output, i.e. K = 2 and L = 2 will produce Q = 200. This fixed proportions relationship is shown in the following table:

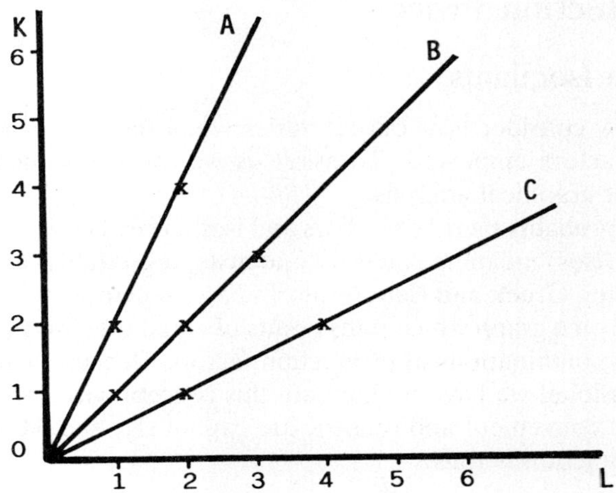

Fig. 2.1 Production Rays
These represent different methods of production using different combinations of capital **K** and labour **L**.

K	*L*	*Q*
1	1	100
2	1	100
3	1	100
1	2	100
1	3	100
2	2	200
3	3	300
4	4	400

The crosses on the production ray B reflect this relationship. If, however, one resource is increased without a proportionate increase in the other then output is limited by the smallest resource. If K = 3 and L = 1 output cannot rise above 100 and two units of capital are wasted.

Fig. 2.2 illustrates an isoquant for this production relationship. An output level of 100 can be produced with one unit of capital and one of labour. Increases in one factor on its own do not result in any increase in output. Fig. 2.2 also shows a section of the isoquant map for this production method. It illustrates combinations of capital and labour producing different levels of output. The further the isoquant from the origin the greater the output level.

Two other production methods are shown in Fig. 2.1. Method A requires factors to be combined in proportions of 2 units of K for each unit

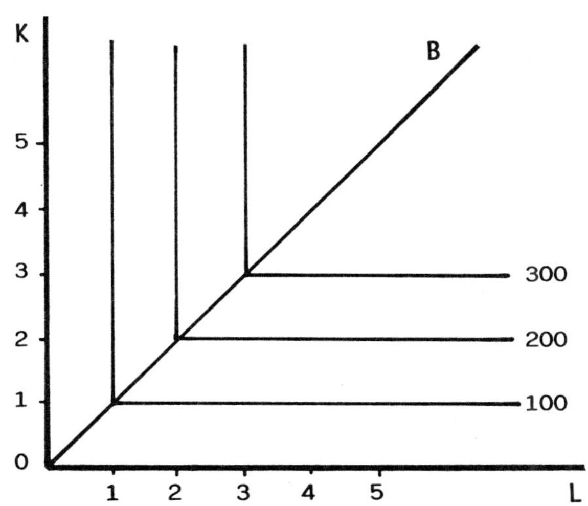

Fig. 2.2 Isoquant associated with production ray of Fig. 2.1
Any factor combination other than 1L + 1K wastes resources.

of L. Method C requires 1K to 2L. Part of a possible output table for these methods might be:

Method A			*Method C*		
K	**L**	**Q**	**K**	**L**	**Q**
2	1	220	1	2	230
4	2	440	2	4	460
6	3	660	3	6	690

In these examples it is assumed that output is produced using only one method of production. The choice has been A, B or C. It is, however, possible to combine the different production methods.

In the following example the firm can use any of three production methods represented by rays X, Y and Z or any combination of these. In method X capital and labour must be used in a ratio of 60K to 1L. Method Y requires 20K to 1L and method Z needs 10K to 2L.

Method X			*Method Y*			*Method Z*		
K	**L**	**Q**	**K**	**L**	**Q**	**K**	**L**	**Q**
30	0.5	100	20	1	100	10	2	100
60	1	200	40	2	200	20	4	200
90	1.5	300	60	3	300	30	6	300

Suppose the firm wished to produce 300 units. It could do so by combining method Y to produce 200 units and Z to produce 100 units. This would require 40K and 2L, using Y and 10K and 2L, using Z, a total of 50K and 4L. This is represented by point R on the 300 isoquant between the rays for methods Y and Z. Try other possible combinations for yourself. You will find that each isoquant is made up of a series of straight line segments representing the possible combinations of methods available.

Continuous substitution of factors

If more production methods (rays) are added to Fig. 2.3 the number of segments to each isoquant increases. The greater the number of production methods, the closer this approaches a curve. The more easily capital and labour can be substituted the smoother the production isoquant becomes. Assume a continuous ability to substitute capital for labour and we have the isoquant shaped as in Fig. 2.4. Although it can be argued that this is less realistic than the position represented by Fig. 2.3, it does have a number of advantages for general analysis. It is more easily handled mathematically, for example, because the smooth curve lends itself to the application of the calculus. Notice the general shape of the curve, convex to the origin. This assumes the existence of an important relationship between factors that can be substituted for each other. As we continue to employ further increments of a factor, the amount of the substitute factor

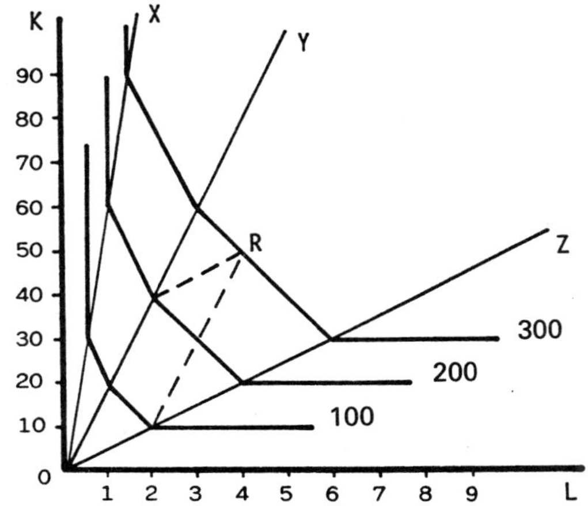

Fig. 2.3 Isoquants representing limited factor substitutability
Production is achieved by any of the ways represented by production rays **X,Y** or **Z** or by a combination of these, such as **R**.

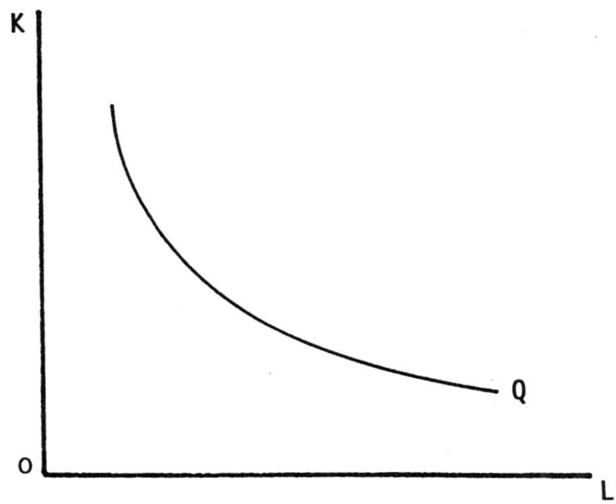

Fig. 2.4 The isoquant illustrating continuous substitutability between labour L and capital K.

that it replaces tends to diminish, assuming that the total level of output is to be maintained.

The rate at which one factor can replace another is known as the **marginal rate of substitution**. Marginal, as explained in the next section, is a term frequently used in economics to refer to changes at the edge or in a total amount. The marginal rate of substitution of labour for capital, then, relates to the increase in labour needed to replace a reduction in capital when the level of output is held constant. We normally expect to find a **diminishing rate of marginal substitution**. This means that the more of one factor that is employed the less of the other is required to provide an adequate substitution. The more machines we are already employing, for example, the less is the reduction in labour needed to compensate for any further increment of capital in the form of additional machinery. Here we are assuming that all other influences, including the level of technology, remain constant. This, as we explain in Chapter 3, is essentially a short-run condition.

The principle is illustrated in Fig. 2.5. Given this isoquant the addition of 1 more unit of capital to an existing 2 units of capital already employed reduces the number of labour units from 11 weekly hours to 8 but when total capital employed has reached 6 units, a further 1 replaces only 1 weekly hour. Total production remains unchanged as all these possible combinations of capital and labour are found on the same isoquant.

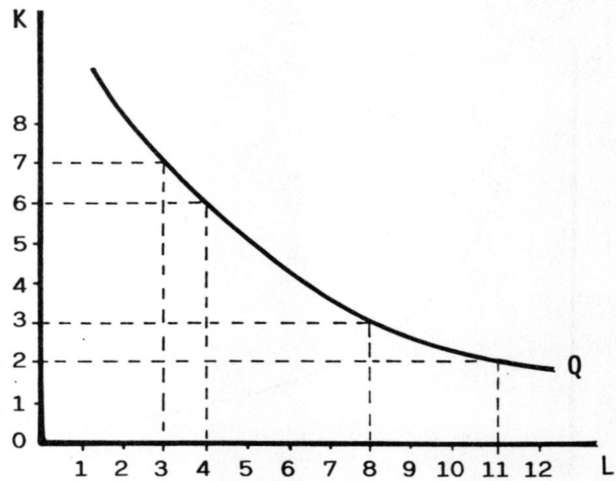

Fig. 2.5 The marginal rate of substitution
The amount of **L** needed to replace 1**K** falls as more **K** is employed.

Resources and Output Changes

The Margin

We are now concerned with changes in total output and this brings us to one of the most important concepts in economics, that of the **margin**, or

marginal change. A marginal change is the extent to which a total quantity of one variable is affected by a very small, usually **a single unit**, change in another variable. The term 'marginal' is used because it concerns movements at the edge of a total. For example, if the weekly total output of a firm rises from 500 to 600 units when an extra worker is employed then the firm's marginal output from employing the worker is 100 units per week. The concept, of course, is by no means unique to economics. Mathematicians will recognise that marginal analysis makes available to economists the very powerful techniques of the differential calculus.

Marginal Product and Short-run Production

The change in total product or output achieved when we change the input of one or more production factors is called the **marginal product**, or more correctly, the **marginal physical product (MPP)** of that factor.

We can first examine the position when at least one factor remains constant and we add more inputs of another factor. For simplicity we can take the case of two factors, capital and labour, and assume that capital is being held constant and labour is being increased. The period during which at least one factor is held constant is known as the **short run** so that we are now examining short-run changes in production.

Consider the following table and graphs of Fig. 2.6.

Labour	*Units of Total physical product of labour*	*Marginal physical product of labour*
0	0	
1	5	5
2	15	10
3	30	15
4	45	15
5	55	10
6	60	5
7	60	0
8	50	−10

The marginal physical product (MPP) represents the gain in total physical product (TPP) resulting from the employment of 1 more unit of labour. For example, the MPP achieved by the sixth unit = the TPP resulting from employing 6 units – the TPP achieved by employing 5. In this table the MPP6 = 60 − 55 = 5.

Fig. 2.6 shows how successive increments of one factor (L) can be expected to affect TPP and MPP when the other factors (K) are held constant. Notice that the marginal values are plotted at the midpoints of each unit change. This is because they relate to the change from one unit to the next.

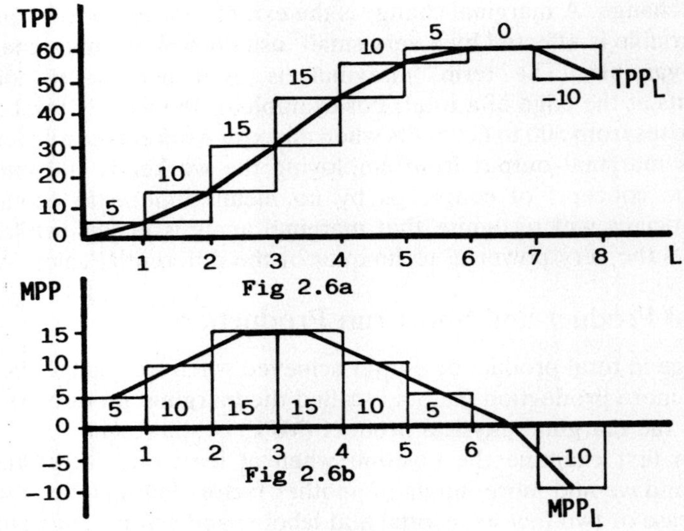

Fig. 2.6 The law of variable proportions
Fig. 2.6a shows increases in total physical product resulting from increasing inputs of labour. Fig. 2.6b shows the marginal physical product and illustrates how **MPP** changes as inputs of L increase, assuming that other factors are held constant.

We expect the increases in output or production (MPP) first to increase, then to stay constant and then to diminish until a maximum total product has been reached. At this point any further increments of labour would actually reduce output. MPP is then negative. This reflects what is usually called the **law of variable proportions.**

This law is not suggesting that later workers employed are any more or less industrious than the others. It is a physical result of changing the proportion of one factor when the quantity employed of the other is held constant. For example, if one person were employed in a small workshop he would have to do everything himself, look after the equipment, fetch and carry all his materials, keep the workshop clean and so on. The arrival of a helper would free him to spend more time operating the equipment. Each worker could specialise in different aspects of the work and so raise the level of their skills. Two workers could thus produce more than twice the output of one. However, an attempt to employ, say, four workers in the same small area with the same machinery could cause problems. They could get in each other's way and even devise additional unproductive tasks just to keep themselves fully occupied. You can think of examples for yourself and also imagine what would happen if more and more machines were acquired without increasing the number of workers to use them.

In practice we are normally less interested in the very low levels of output where MPP is increasing than in the higher levels where it is diminishing. In this example, the MPP of labour is diminishing from the employment of the fifth unit, illustrating what is frequently known as the **law of diminishing marginal returns** of a variable factor. Labour here is the variable factor because changes in output are the result of changes in the number of units of labour employed. We would not, of course, expect the rational firm to employ labour beyond the point of maximum total product.

A diminishing marginal physical product for labour implies that a constant increment of labour will result in a rising total product but that the amount of successive product rises will diminish. This is illustrated in Fig. 2.7 where the horizontal line represents the fixed quantity of capital, labour units are plotted on the horizontal axis, and the isoquants represent the total output quantities of Fig. 2.6.

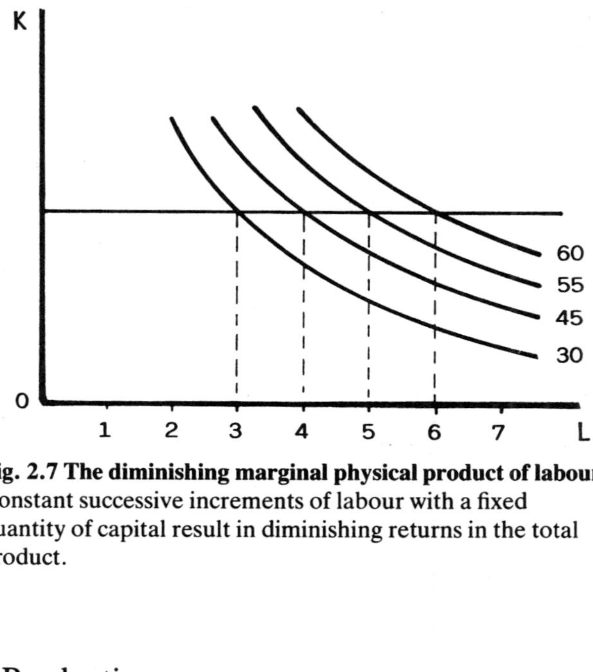

Fig. 2.7 The diminishing marginal physical product of labour
Constant successive increments of labour with a fixed quantity of capital result in diminishing returns in the total product.

Long-run Production

In the short run at least one factor, usually capital, is held constant. In **the long run all factors become variable** and may be increased in order to achieve increased levels of output. In this long-run period, factors may be changed in the same proportion or in different proportions. Studies at this level normally concentrate on changes of factors in the same proportion and the term **returns to scale** refers to output increase achieved in this way.

Returns to Scale

The returns to scale are the output increases that result from increasing all factor inputs in proportion. They can be constant, increasing, or decreasing.

Constant returns to scale
This is the condition that we might expect to double the size of the product if we double the input of ingredients. However, if you have any knowledge of the laws of physics you will know that this constant relationship between input and output will not always hold good.

Increasing returns to scale
The term 'mass production' is a familiar one. It refers to the employment of production processes that are only available for very large levels of output. It is only worth while setting up a motor vehicle assembly line costing millions of pounds when a mass market for standard vehicles exists. Once a given level of production is achieved this may be increased with very few additional inputs, e.g., by running the line a little faster. However, it is unlikely to be possible to halve production by halving the inputs. Large-scale machinery is often 'indivisible'. Specialised management usually has similar qualities of indivisibility. As more efficient use is made of such managers, output can be increased more than proportionally to factor inputs.

Decreasing returns to scale
While management can produce increasing returns it is also a common cause of decreasing returns. As organisations grow large there tend to arise problems of managerial coordination. Decision making becomes more formalised and communication systems less efficient. There may also be physical barriers to continually increasing output by increasing the size and quantity of inputs.

It should be noted that these production economies of scale are all **internal** to the firm. They exist because of qualities relating to the large production plant. Some other features of large-scale production and of certain possible external factors together with their implications for business costs are examined in the next chapter.

Exercises Relating to Chapter 2

1 Identify the production factors likely to be employed by firms producing household furniture. Explain the rewards applicable to these factors. What differences might there be between a large and a small organisation?

2 Suppose there are three possible production methods for manufacturing a product. One uses capital and labour in the ratio of 2:1 (physical factor units), the second in the ratio of 3:1 and the third in the ratio of 4:1. The machinery is such that any departure from these ratios results in a waste of resources but it is possible to employ both the second and third methods in the same factory.

Draw suitable production rays and isoquants to represent this situation and show how two different production levels can be achieved.

3 Complete the following table.

Units of labour	*Units of total physical product*	*Marginal physical product*
1	30	
2	37	7
3	45	
4	53	
5		8
6	67	
7		5
8	76	

What economic 'law' is illustrated by this table? What conditions are necessary for this law to apply? Why would you not expect it to apply in the long run?

3

The costs of production

Short-run Costs

Costs and Output

In Chapter 2 we defined the short run as that period during which one or more production factors do not change in quantity as production levels change. Notice that the important relationship is to a range of output rather than just to a period of time, although the two are likely to be linked.

We have suggested that, as long as some factors, say land and capital, remain fixed then the producer is likely to experience first increasing, then constant and finally diminishing returns. This means that a constant increase in the input of a variable factor will produce first a rising, then a constant and eventually a falling marginal output.

Instead of seeing this in terms of changing marginal product, we can consider the implications for changes in costs as production is increased. In Chapter 2 we explained that when a firm employs production factors it has to pay the appropriate factor rewards. These payments are the costs incurred by the firm to achieve production. A change in total cost resulting from a change in the total output level is a change at the margin. It is the *marginal cost* which we can, then, define as the change in total cost resulting from a very small, or unit, change in quantity produced. Notice the similarity with marginal physical product (MPP) as this was defined in Chapter 2.

If we think in terms of a constant increment in output then the marginal costs of achieving this must depend on the quantity of factor inputs required. Constant marginal returns imply that inputs are in constant proportion to output. Marginal costs, therefore, must also be constant. Increasing returns imply that inputs are added in a smaller proportion than the additions to output so marginal costs must fall as output rises. On the other hand, **diminishing returns** have the opposite effect and must bring about **rising marginal costs**.

This can be illustrated by a simple example. Suppose we have an organisation where capital and land are held constant and the only variable factor input is labour, a service organisation perhaps, not using any basic resources.

The cost of the fixed factor inputs will not change as the volume of output changes. Capital (K) and land (S), therefore, give rise to **fixed costs**. The cost of labour (L), however will change as output changes. Labour is the variable factor and gives rise to **variable costs**.

Suppose we can measure both the labour input and the production output in units. If we increase the labour input a unit at a time, the result might be as shown in the following table.

Note the abbreviations used for the column headings:

L = units of labour
TPPL = total physical product resulting from the employment of a given quantity of labour
MPPL = marginal physical product of labour (additional units of output produced by each successive unit of labour employed)
PL = unit price of labour
MCP = marginal cost of product. This is the change in total labour cost divided by the change in the TPPL. Here it is found by dividing the price of one unit of labour by the MPP of that unit (PL ÷ MPPL). It is, therefore, an average and as such, an approximation.

1	2	3	4	5
L	TPPL	MPPL	PL	MCP
		Δ2		4 ÷ 3
units	units	units	£	£
0	0		1000	
		100		10.0
1	100		1000	
		133		7.5
2	233		1000	
		167		6.0
3	400		1000	
		200		5.0
4	600		1000	
		200		5.0
5	800		1000	
		200		5.0
6	1000		1000	
		150		6.7
7	1150		1000	
		50		20.0
8	1200		1000	
		25		40.0
9	1225		1000	
		0		∞
10	1225		1000	

The symbol Δ (Greek delta) is frequently used to mean 'a change in' and here it refers to the change from one level to the next in TPPL. Notice that as the price of each unit of labour (think of this as a 'bundle' of man-hours if you wish) stays the same, the cost of the output added by each worker depends upon how much extra output he (or she) contributes. The rational firm will not employ the tenth worker whatever his wage. Remember that this change in the production or output achieved per worker is no reflection on his or her personal qualities. It is the consequence of the law of variable proportions explained in the previous chapter.

It is useful to know the cost implications of employing additional (or fewer) workers. We also often wish to know the cost consequences of changing output levels. To do this, using the same example, we must change the first column from units of labour to units of output. To avoid complications and to keep the figures simple, we have assumed that labour units are divisible where 'intermediate' levels of output have to be estimated. The following table, then, is based on the previous figures and it uses the following abbreviations:

Q = units of output or TPP
AVC = average variable cost, found by dividing the cost of the units of labour needed for a particular output level by the units of output at that level; e.g. 5 labour units produce 800 product units, each labour unit costs £1000, so AVC = £5000 ÷ 800 = £6.25
FC = the unchanging cost of the fixed factors of capital and labour, here assumed to be £2000
TC = the total of fixed and variable costs at the relevant output level
ATC = TC ÷ Q
MC = marginal cost, which is the change in the total cost brought about by a unit change in the output level; in this example, the first column moves in steps of 100 units, the corresponding steps in total costs are divided by 100 to give marginal cost

You should compare the two tables and see how the constant marginal costs result directly from the constant returns achieved by the fourth, fifth and sixth labour units to be employed. As output rises from 400 to 1000 units then marginal costs are also constant.

Average and Marginal Costs

Both tables give us a number of concepts but in particular they introduce two very important cost measures. It is essential to have a clear understanding of average and marginal costs.

Average cost

This term is often used to describe what is more properly the average total cost. It is found by adding the fixed costs (FC) of column 3 to the total variable costs (TVC), the product of AVC (column 2) and Q (column 1) at a given point of output and dividing the total by the output (Q) at that level. Thus:

$$ATC = \frac{FC + TVC}{Q}$$

1	2	3	4	5	6
Q	**AVC**	**FC**	**TC**	**ATC**	**MC**
			(1 × 2) + 3	**4 ÷ 1**	**ΔTC ÷ΔQ**
Units	**£**	**£**	**£**	**£**	**£**
0	0	0	0	0	
100	10.00	2000	3 000	30.00	30.00
200	8.57	2000	3 714	18.57	7.14
300	7.92	2000	4 376	14.58	6.62
400	7.50	2000	5 000	12.50	6.24
500	7.00	2000	5 500	11.00	5.00
600	6.67	2000	6 000	10.00	5.00
700	6.43	2000	6 500	9.29	5.00
800	6.25	2000	7 000	8.75	5.00
900	6.11	2000	7 500	8.33	5.00
1000	6.00	2000	8 000	8.00	5.00
1100	6.06	2000	8 667	7.88	6.67
1200	6.67	2000	10 000	8.33	13.33

Marginal cost

This is the change in total cost resulting from a small change in the level of output. When output changes in larger steps – as in our example – what we really have to find is the average change in cost from one level to another (TC ÷ Q). When we plot this on a graph we plot marginal cost at the midpoint between the two output levels because it represents the change from one to the other. The tables also show this. Mathematicians will recognise marginal cost as the first derivative of total cost with respect to changes in output i.e. dC/dQ where C = total cost and Q = total ouput. Fig. 3.1 shows the average total costs and the marginal costs for the table. Fig. 3.2 shows the normal shapes of all the average cost curves used by economists, together with the marginal cost curve. You should check the shape of the average fixed cost curve for yourself. Divide the fixed costs of £2000 by each quantity level from 100 to 1200. The average variable cost curve approximates to the appropriate table column. You should also understand the various relationships existing between these curves.

Notice that the marginal cost curves **always** cuts the lowest point of the average total cost curve and the average variable cost curve. You can test this statement for yourself. Take any set of figures, find the simple average, add one more figure and find the new average. If the last figure added is more than the first average then the second average will be higher than the first. If the last figure added is lower than the first average then the second average will be lower. Only when the last 'marginal' addition is the same as the first average will this remain unchanged and neither rise nor fall.

Return now to the table of costs. If you have remembered our definition

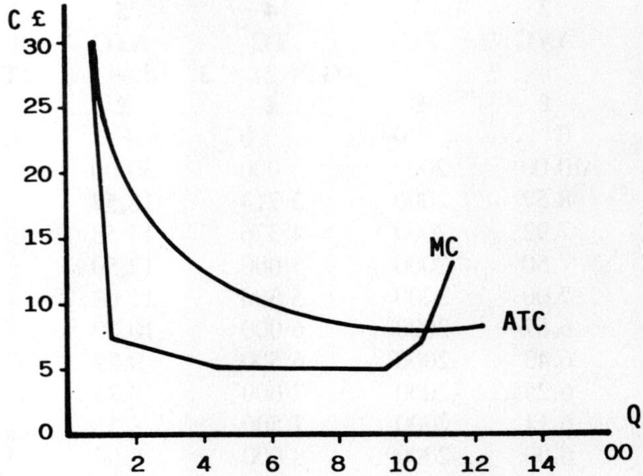

Fig. 3.1 Average, total and marginal costs
These curves are based on the cost table. Notice how the **MC** curve cuts the **ATC** curve at its minimum point.

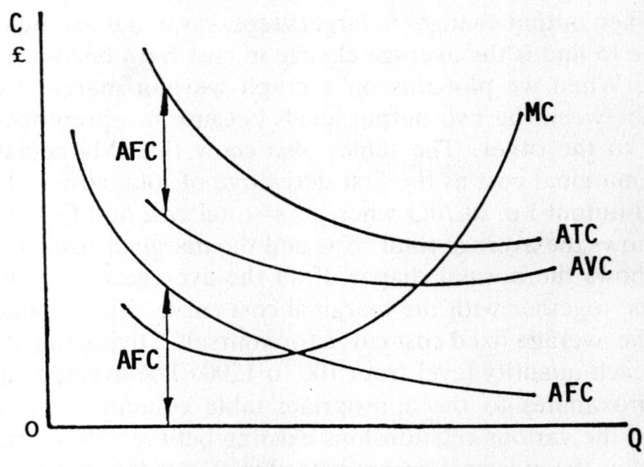

Fig. 3.2 The way economists like to draw cost curves

of short- and long-run production you will realise that what the table shows is a short-run condition. At the output level of 1200 units the marginal costs are rising steeply, reflecting the steep fall in extra production achieved from further inputs of labour. At this stage the firm has clearly reached the limits of feasible production with its existing fixed quantities of land and capital.

Long-run Costs

Increasing Fixed Factors

If our imaginary firm wishes to increase output further it must introduce more of the fixed factors. It may decide to do this by acquiring more machinery and so increase the input of physical capital. Suppose it does so at an output level of 1200 units and, as a result, raises its fixed costs to £3000. At the same time the additional capital allows new and more efficient techniques to be used and enables the firm to reduce variable costs to a level below that achieved under the old fixed costs. Suppose it is able to record average variable costs of £5 per unit of output levels up to 1500 but at output levels above 1500 units these start to rise again.

The new position is illustrated in the next table which uses the same columns and abbreviations as before. Notice that the change has enabled the firm to reduce average total costs below the level achieved with the smaller production unit. It has also enabled the firm to reduce average costs and, as we shall see later, this figure is crucial for choosing the best profit output level. Had the increase not been made the marginal and average total costs would have climbed steeply and the firm would not have been able to expand output any further.

The effect of the change in the quantity of fixed factors employed is further illustrated in the graph of Fig. 3.3 where we see a fall in average costs, followed by a renewed rise as diminishing returns re-emerge.

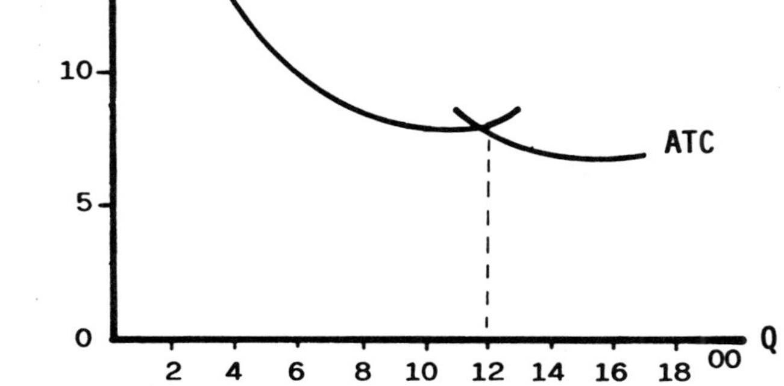

Fig. 3.3 Average total costs when fixed costs are increased
This graph is based on the cost table showing a rise in fixed costs from £2000 to £3000.

1 Q Units	2 AVC £	3 FC £	4 TC £	5 ATC £	6 MC £
1100	6.06	2000	8 667	7.88	
1200	6.67	2000	10 000	8.33	13.33
1100	5.75	3000	9 325	8.48	13.25
1200	5.50	3000	9 600	8.00	2.75
1300	5.30	3000	9 890	7.61	2.90
1400	5.13	3000	10 182	7.27	2.92
1500	5.00	3000	10 500	7.00	3.18
1600	5.00	3000	11 000	6.87	5.00
1700	5.00	3000	11 500	6.76	5.00
1800	5.25	3000	12 450	6.92	9.50
1900	5.50	3000	13 450	7.08	10.00

Suppose the firm continues with these fixed factor injections. Over the long-period its average total costs may look something like Fig. 3.4. This assumes a continuation of the process illustrated in Fig. 3.3 as output continues to increase. Each level where the short-run cost curves intersect represents a stage when the firm has to make the difficult decision whether or not to raise its production capacity by introducing new inputs of a fixed factor such as capital.

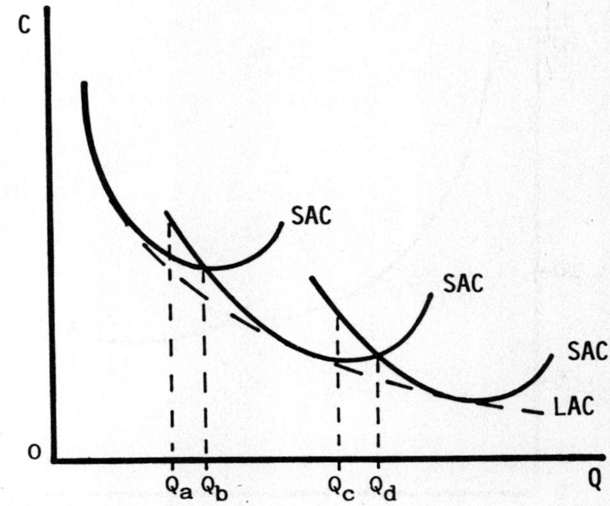

Fig. 3.4 The long-run average cost curve
Continued inputs of fixed production factors enable the firm to keep reducing average total costs.

If, on the assumption that the fixed factor, capital (K), can be increased in small quantities, we smooth out the curve, as indicated by the dotted line, we produce what is usually known as the L-shaped long-run average cost curve. This, it is often argued, is more realistic for the modern firm than the U-shaped curve accepted as a portrayal of the short run. We might also think of the long-run curve as an indication of the planning problem faced by the firm. The firm has to decide whether demand justifies building a larger plant. Remember that once the additional fixed costs have been incurred they cannot be removed. If demand falls back and the firm has to produce at a falling level of output it will be faced with the steeply rising curve shown in Fig. 3.4 between Q_a and Q_b and also between Q_c and Q_d. The intersection of the alternative short-run curves illustrates the choice that has to be made by the firm at these critical levels of output. The general shape of the curve assumes that the firm is able to obtain continuing benefits from introducing improved machines and production methods and so to overcome the short-run effects of diminishing marginal returns. These benefits are examined further in the next section.

Long-run Economies of Scale

The possibility that the firm could obtain economies in the use of production factors as it increased in size was introduced in the previous chapter. We now examine this in more detail. There are two types of economies which may be achieved. These are pecuniary or monetary economies, and real economies.

Pecuniary economies

These are money savings from purchasing factors at reduced cost. They do not represent a more efficient use of factors but do, of course, produce a cost reduction for the firm. Large firms, for example, are often able to use their market power to gain special discounts from suppliers. Workers are sometimes willing to accept a lower wage from a large firm which is believed to offer some security of employment and also a degree of social prestige.

Real economies

Real economies refer to genuine efficiencies in the use of production factors. Consequently, greater output can be achieved from a given quantity of factors as the size of the plant increases. A wide range of these economies have been identified. They include the following:

1 **Labour economies** These result from greater opportunities for the division of labour which increase the skills of the workforce, save time and permit greater mechanisation. At an extreme level these processes have led to the automation of the assembly line for mass-produced goods

and massive increases in the output that can be achieved per each worker employed.

2 **Technical economies** These result largely from the use of specialised capital equipment. In the previous chapter we noted how indivisibilities of some capital equipment made possible the economies of large scale production. Large firms are also able to support reserve machines to avoid disruption following breakdown. A small firm using one machine will double its capital costs if it tries to have a spare machine. A large firm using 20 machines will only add one twentieth if it keeps an additional one in reserve.

3 **Marketing economies** There are very substantial economies in large scale advertising. One television advertising film can cost some thousands of pounds but, with little alteration it can be shown in America, the UK, through most of Western Europe and possibly in some Far Eastern countries. For companies able to afford the high initial expense the final 'exposure cost' (cost per potential buyer actually seeing the advertisement) is very small. Large companies can afford first-class market research and employ highly skilled marketing specialists. The result is to achieve greater certainty in estimating demand, in pricing products and in producing products that will appeal to changing markets.

4 **Financial economies** Large firms have access to sources of finance that are denied to small firms. The administrative costs of raising money from the public are very heavy and can only be justified if the amount to be raised is also very large. Although these economies certainly exist we should be aware that financial services available to small firms have been much improved during the 1970s and 1980s.

5 **Distribution and transport economies** Large firms can plan the location of depots and the distribution of goods so that vehicles are used efficiently and stocks kept at efficient levels. Planning transport networks presents interesting mathematical problems but only large firms can take advantage of savings that can be achieved by their solution.

6 **Managerial Economies** These arise from the employment of specialised managers and from the mechanisation of communications and the more routine aspects of decision making. Managerial economies have given rise to more discussion and controversy than any other group and some writers argue that the large firm is more likely to suffer from managerial diseconomies than to enjoy managerial economies. A few economists suggest that there comes a point in the growth of the firm when managerial diseconomies and inefficiencies will more than offset any other economies. At this stage the long-run average cost curve will begin to rise. Other writers dispute this. While there is no doubt that all large organisations suffer from managerial problems from time to time these

are likely to be overcome and cause only a temporary check to continued growth and further scale economies.

External Economies

As pointed out earlier these are all economies that are internal to the large firm and they give it advantages over smaller firms. There are further economies that are **external** to the firm and which arise when an industry grows large or when industrial firms congregate in a particular area. External economies usually involve the development of specialised services available to many firms. For example an area containing numbers of small engineering companies may provide sufficient work to support one or more firms of specialised toolmakers. Each engineering company can call on a specialised toolmaker without having to bear the expense of setting up a costly specialist department. If, however, one or two of the companies grow to a dominating size they may internalise these economies by developing toolmaking departments. The surviving small companies may not be able to provide enough work to sustain the independent specialist firms and without their services the engineers find it increasingly difficult to compete with the dominant companies.

Factor Choice and Cost

Factor Substitution

In Chapter 2 we saw how the producer could vary his mixture of factor inputs – the ingredients of his finished product – as well as the quantity of all factors employed. One resource may replace another. Plastics may substitute for metals; labour and capital can be combined in various ways. The computer exercise uses a simple example of digging holes employing several combinations of capital and labour. It is not difficult to think of others. An 'office services' firm progressing from manual to electric and then to electronic typewriters and word processors would be changing its ratio of labour to capital employed. It would also, one hopes, be changing its possible total output.

Business management at all levels is very much concerned with choosing the 'best' mixture of factor inputs. If economics is concerned with all aspects of choosing scarce resources to meet human needs then we would look to economic analysis to have developed some tools to help us understand this area of decision making.

We must recognize that many problems relevant to factor substitution are fairly complex and we should not expect to find a complete guide to business managerial economics in a few printed pages and computer exercises. At this stage of study we must be satisfied to gain some basic techniques and concepts. Having mastered these, however distant they may seem from practical business problems, we shall have secured a sure basis for further study and deeper understanding.

Choice and Cost

If the producer does have the choice of varying combinations of capital and labour, or indeed any other two inputs to the production process, there remains the problem of how to choose the best combination.

We now examine this problem and assume, at this stage, that the firm's aim is to achieve a desired level of production or output at the lowest possible (minimum) cost. This, in turn, will depend upon the rate at which capital and labour can be substituted for each other, indicated by the shape of the isoquant, as explained in Chapter 2. It will also depend upon the costs of each factor.

Suppose that the hourly labour cost is £6 and the hourly cost of employing capital is £1. Its available budget for spending on labour and capital is £90. It must now decide its most favourable combination of labour and capital. Suppose that the £90 could be used entirely on labour, entirely on capital or on any possible combination of these which together total £90. All the possible combinations occur on the line AB in Fig. 3.5.

You will not be surprised to learn that AB, representing all combinations of the two factors which have the same total cost, is called an **isocost** line or curve. Remember that the mathematical term 'curve' includes straight lines or 'linear' curves.

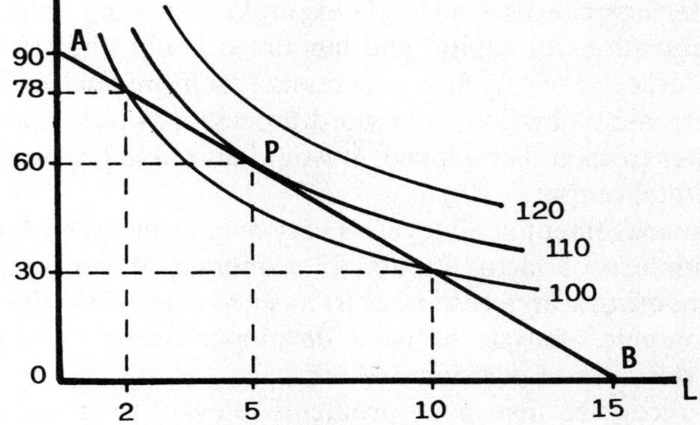

Fig. 3.5 The best combination of production factors
Given the factor costs represented by the isocost line **AB**, the best factor combination is **P** (60K + 5L) which just attains production level **110**.

The line AB extends from 90 capital units (K) representing spending on physical capital (machines, equipment, etc.) alone, to 15 hours of work, representing spending on labour alone. Fig. 3.5 also shows three isoquants representing output levels 100, 110 and 120 from a possible isoquant map. Three out of all the possible combinations of capital (K) and labour (L) are shown in the graph. These are 78K + 2L; 30K + 10L; and finally, point P, representing 60K + 5L. All these 'factor mixes' cost the same amount, £90, but the first produces a production level of 100, whereas point P occurs where the cost line AB is tangential to the higher production isoquant of representing 110. A budget limited to £90 will not allow the firm to reach the 120 production level. Assuming that the firm wishes to reach the **highest attainable level of production** the firm should employ the 'mix' represented by point P.

In any situation where the choice to be made involves two inputs or 'bundles' of inputs at known cost, and where the production conditions are also known, the highest output for a given cost – or the least cost to achieve a given output – will be found at the point where the isocost curve just touches (is tangential, or at a tangent to) the isoquant. Maximum output, therefore, will always occur when an isoquant is at a tangent to an isocost line.

At this point, the ratio of the marginal physical product of labour (MPPL) to the price of labour (PL) is equal to the ratio of the marginal physical product of capital (MPPK) to the price of capital (PK). This proposition is very important and we need to understand it clearly.

We have already shown that an isoquant represents different combinations of labour and capital which can produce the same output level. Let us examine what happens when we move from one point (A) to another (B) along an isoquant. This is represented in Fig. 3.6.

Some Implications of Choice Analysis

Such a move entails reducing the amount of capital used. This is represented by ΔK. The Greek symbol Δ is frequently employed to mean 'a change in'. If we simply reduce K by a given amount there will be a loss of output. The loss (or gain) resulting from a reduction (or increase) in the quantity of K by one unit is the marginal physical product of capital (MPPK). Thus, ΔK units of K lead to an output loss of $\Delta K \times MPPK$.

By moving from A to B along the same isoquant we are not just reducing K but replacing it by an increase in L and the amount of L needed to make good the fall in K is ΔL. Following the same argument as that of the previous paragraph, the gain in output from increasing L is $\Delta L \times MPPL$ and, because the total output is unchanged, this equals the loss from reducing K. One change simply cancels out the other. This can be expressed very simply in the form:

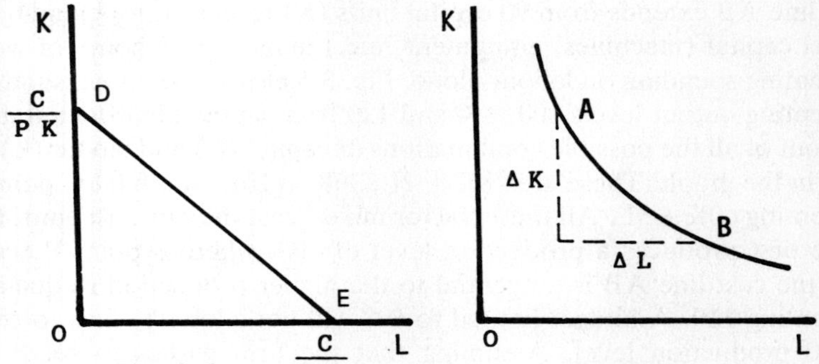

Fig 3.6a

Fig 3.6b

Fig. 3.6 Movement along an isoquant and the best output conditions
Movement from **A** to **B** in Fig. 3.6b involves replacing some **K** (**ΔK**) by some **L** (**ΔL**) but total production is unchanged. At the best production point the isocost line of Fig. 3.6a is tangential to the isoquant.

$$\Delta K \cdot MPPK + \Delta L \cdot MPPL = 0$$

From this we see that:

$$\frac{\Delta K}{\Delta L} = \frac{-MPPL}{MPPK} = \text{the slope of the isoquant}$$

Now examine the isocost line shown in Fig. 3.6a. The budget available for spending on both factor inputs is C. Point D, where the whole budget is spent on K is, of course, C ÷ PK (where PK is the unit price of capital). Similarly, point E is C ÷ PL (where PL is the unit price of labour). The slope of the isocost line is thus:

$$\frac{C \div PK}{C \div PL} = \frac{-PL}{PK}$$

At the point of tangency the slopes of the isoquant and the isocost curves must be equal. Thus:

$$\frac{MPPL}{MPPK} = \frac{PL}{PK} \quad \text{and} \quad \frac{MPPK}{PK} = \frac{MPPL}{PL}$$

This simply means that the cost minimising producer will seek to ensure that the last £ spent on capital will achieve the same additional product as the last £ spent on labour. If this were not the case it would pay him to change his mixture of capital and labour. If the marginal product per £ of capital were greater than that of labour so that:

$$\frac{MPPK}{PK} > \frac{MPPL}{PL}$$

then, given that diminishing marginal returns apply, the producer should increase his employment of capital and/or reduce his employment of labour until the marginal product of labour rises sufficiently to bring about equality in the required relationships.

Consider the following example where:

the marginal physical product of capital = 400
the unit price of capital = 20
the marginal physical product of labour = 18
the unit price of labour = 1 then:

$$\frac{MPPK}{PK} = \frac{400}{20} > \frac{MPPL}{PL} = \frac{18}{1}$$

Assuming that diminishing marginal returns apply, the producer should increase his employment of capital and/or reduce his employment of labour until the marginal product of capital falls and/or the marginal product of labour rises sufficiently to bring about equality in the required relationships.

Suppose we transfer £20 from labour to capital. We lose 360 output units from labour (18×20) but gain 400 units from the increased capital. It would pay the firm to do this because there is a net gain of 40 units of output. It would, therefore, continue to substitute capital for labour until the ratios of marginal physical products and prices were equal. Substitution would, of course, change the marginal physical products. Remember the law of diminishing marginal returns outlined in Chapter 2. As more capital is employed, the marginal physical product of capital will fall. As less labour is employed, its marginal physical product will rise.

You may be regarding this analysis as all very theoretical and abstract, and be wondering what, if any, significance it may have to the real world. However, consider the following statements:

1 Between 1975 and 1980, the average wage rate in British industry rose faster than the rise in marginal productivity of labour so that the wage cost per unit of physical product rose.
2 Over the same period, there were considerable improvements in technology and reductions in the cost of electronic equipment.
3 From around 1980, labour unemployment in the UK started to rise steeply.

It would, of course, be foolish to think that these statements give anything like a full explanation of the unemployment of the 1980s. Nevertheless, it would be equally foolish to ignore the need of producers to choose the most effective combinations of production inputs and to replace one factor by another following changes in relative factor costs.

Another issue to which this type of analysis is relevant is that of the distribution of industry in different areas of the world. Wage and capital costs differ in different countries and these differences help to explain the movement of major industries from one country to another. We have to remember, however, that it is the ratio of marginal physical product to factor price and not factor price alone that is important. Wages can rise without harming the prospects for employment if the marginal physical product of labour rises sufficiently to maintain, or even improve, its ratio to the marginal productivity of capital.

Exercises Relating to Chapter 3

1 What is the marginal cost of labour? Refer to the table of question 3 in Chapter 2. Assuming that each unit of labour costs £2000, prepare an additional column to show the marginal cost of labour.

2 What is the marginal cost of production? How does it differ from average total cost of production? Using the table produced for question 1, add a further column to show the marginal cost of production. Assuming that there is a constant capital cost of £5000, calculate the average total cost column. Graph the following curves from the figures of your complete table: **a** average fixed cost; **b** average total cost; **c** marginal cost of production. What is the relationship between **b** and **c**?

3 A well known modern economist has commented that it is the function of the business manager to 'flatten the U shaped cost curve'. Explain as fully as you can how the manager can achieve this in the long run. What are the implications of his success in doing so?

4 The following table shows how labour (L), and capital (K), can be combined to produce a product (X).

Production level 700 units		**Production level 900 units**	
L (units)	**K (units)**	**L (units)**	**K (units)**
11	3	11	5
9	4	9	6
7	5	7	7
6	6	6	8
4	9	5	10
3	12	4	13

Given that the unit cost of labour is £4 and of capital £3 and that the budget available is £48, what production level would you advise and what combination of labour and capital? Support your answer with a graphical illustration.

What would be the effect of a rise in the unit cost of capital to £4, all other conditions remaining unchanged? Discuss your conclusions.

5 In the light of the isocost/isoquant analysis of Chapter 2 would you expect developing countries to use similar production techniques to those employed in the advanced industrial countries when producing goods such as motor or agricultural vehicles?

4

Firms, industries and supply

Organisational Objectives

Private Sector Organisations

In Chapter 2 we outlined a range of different organisational structures which together made up the production side of the economy. It would be surprising if the different types of producers did not also have different objectives. This may seem a strange statement when 'traditional' economics is often criticised for seeming to assume that, for the private sector, there is only one goal, that of profit maximisation.

We must be careful to recognise what this implies. Profit maximisation means that the largest possible profit is being sought. In modern economics it is frequently argued that we should not assume profit maximisation to be the only or even the most important goal, and that attention must be paid to other objectives.

This argument is more than just an interesting academic debate. The objectives of the firm influence policies for such important decision making areas as pricing, investment, advertising and labour relations. These decisions affect the public directly as consumers and indirectly through the use – or misuse – of scarce resources. They also help to determine the general level and pattern of economic activity and interact with government economic policies. Without a clear understanding of business objectives, therefore, any study of the economy is likely to have serious weaknesses.

Accepting this view does not mean that we no longer pay any attention to profit maximising conditions. Nor does it mean that we should abandon the whole body of analytical reasoning that has grown up around profit maximising principles. The traditional framework of analysis remains important for a number of very good reasons:

1 Any assumption based on the optimisation or maximisation of an objective lends itself to precise and powerful mathematical analysis, and helps us to master techniques which are essential for further study into 'more realistic' and certainly more complex assumptions.

2 Profit maximisation is especially useful because it takes into account both costs and revenues and leads to more thorough investigation of these than would be likely to follow from other assumptions of business aims. In particular, it leads to a careful analysis of marginal conditions which are of great importance to business decision making.
3 Even if we accept that, in practice, business firms, especially the large firms of the corporate sector, pursue aims other than profit maximisation there should still be an awareness by managers and others of the cost in terms of profit sacrificed of the pursuit of these other objectives. Notice how we tend to come back to the concept of **opportunity cost**.
4 In some market structures, as we shall see, profit maximisation can be a condition for the survival of the firm, whether the business owners consciously pursue it or not. Consequently, under conditions approaching these structures, the business owner who understands what is involved in profit maximisation has a greater chance of success.
5 A number of managerial practices can turn out, on close analysis, to look remarkably like practical approximations to profit maximisation. If successful business managers are profit maximising accidentally, they might be even more successful if they had a better awareness of the scientific or mathematical rules they were unwittingly obeying. Think of the great improvement in sporting performances achieved through the application of improved scientific knowledge to individual physical training. This, at least, suggests that improved economic knowledge might be a useful addition to business training.

If, however, we admit to other business aims then these must be identified. A number have been suggested. To follow through the implications of some of these requires economic analysis beyond the level of introductory studies. At this stage we simply list some of the main possibilities.

Revenue (sales) maximisation
This is one of the simplest of what are often called the managerial theories of the firm. Revenue is seen as tangible evidence of growth or business expansion. As such it is considered to be desirable by 'professional' business managers. The requirements for achieving revenue maximisation and the conditions where it is most likely to occur are examined more fully in Chapter 9. An understanding of these propositions is tested in a number of the computer exercises in the monopoly and competition section and in the game BOTCH UPS.

Pursuit of growth
This is not quite the same as revenue maximisation and does not lend itself to such neat and precise analysis. It is, however, a recognition of the importance of expansion to the modern company. As in the case of revenue maximisation, those who believe that firms pursue growth

maximisation agree that managers will first have to achieve and maintain a minimum profit as required by financial markets before seeking growth.

Managerial utility
This may sound rather vague but, in fact, has a fairly precise meaning and recognises that managers derive satisfaction from the **growth** of the enterprise especially the expansion of their authority over people, from **profits** above the minimum required to satisfy financial markets, and from the enjoyment of those **emoluments or perks** of managerial office that are evident enough to anyone travelling first class by rail or air.

Satisficing
This rather ugly word recognises that managers may not be able to maximise anything, but are entirely engaged in seeking compromises to a set of conflicting and developing aims. The best the manager can hope to achieve is a reasonable measure of consensus from the conflicting but allied participants who form the modern corporate enterprise. The satisficing view of managerial decision making is given a formal and influential expression in the writings of Simon and in the behavioural theory of the firm developed by Cyert and March.

Objectives of Public Sector Organisations

Clarifying the objectives of the industrial and commercial organisations of the public sector can be even less certain than in the private sector. Introductory textbooks used to contain statements to the effect that nationalised industries did not have to pursue profits and were free to operate in the 'public interest'. Unfortunately such statements are not very helpful. There is not one public interest but many. Users of public services want low prices; taxpayers want to avoid losses that have to be made good from taxation; workers and managers want high personal rewards and freedom from the pressures of competition. Managers may also pursue empire building and growth objectives in much the same way as their counterparts in the private, corporate sector. It has been claimed that managers of some nationalised industries have achieved independence from the control of Government and Parliament in much the same way as managers in large companies have gained freedom from shareholder control.

Successive governments in the UK have recognised the problem and a series of White (Policy Statement) Papers, issued in 1961, 1967 and 1978, have attempted to give the public corporations controlling the nationalised industries clearer and firmer financial objectives. The need to ensure that the scarce resources devoted to the nationalised industries achieve a financial return comparable to investments in the private sector has been stated and translated into financial targets.

At the same time, the financial objectives of the White Papers have continually been frustrated by governments which have used the public sector enterprises as vehicles of their own wider economic and political objectives. At various times, these have included prices and wages controls and restraints, restrictions on borrowing and the maintenance of employment in sensitive political regions. Economic and political objectives have constantly been interwoven throughout the history of the nationalised industries.

The latest attempts to 'privatise' (return to the private sector) state enterprises seems unlikely to be a solution for more than a few individual activities. Few private investors are anxious to risk capital in the more difficult and unprofitable areas of the public sector. This was shown clearly in the Government's failure to sell shares in Britoil when these were issued in 1982.

Nevertheless, clear objectives are probably more important for public sector activities than for those in the private sector. The behaviour of a police force will be very different if its objective is stated to be to 'prevent crime' from another force with the objective to 'catch criminals'. You can apply similar reasoning to the objectives of health and fire services! You might also ask several teachers what they consider to be the objectives of a school or college.

The Firm and the Industry

The Firm and the Market Environment

The firm does not exist in isolation. It produces goods and services to meet wants. The wishes of producers to supply goods and services must interact with the willingness of consumers to sacrifice resources (represented by money) to obtain them. How this results in a price and market system is examined later. At this stage we recognise that the extent of consumer demand must influence the volume of production which can be supplied to the market.

We can, therefore, identify a number of influences likely to determine the volume of production open to the firm.

Market size

A market can be defined as an area within which the buyers and sellers of a particular 'economic good' can communicate and trade with each other. The term 'economic good' is convenient when we wish it to apply very widely. It includes any physical product, service or factor of production whose use necessitates some payment in scarce resources. The size of any given market depends on the strength of demand – people buy more toothpaste than they do toothbrushes, for example – and on the effectiveness of transport and communications. Most consumer markets are now international; you are probably wearing at least one article made in another country.

Technical barriers to market entry
If manufacture involves a very heavy expenditure in capital goods, or if large scale production based on a high ratio of capital to labour enables production to take place at a unit price (average total cost) very much lower than small-scale production, the producers are likely to be large firms. The 'entry cost' can be very high indeed for some markets, eg oil exploration and extraction, and motor vehicle or aircraft manufacture. When the amount of capital required is high, the average total cost curve is heavily influenced by the element of average fixed costs (AFC). Fig. 4.1 shows the curve produced when a total cost of £1000 is divided by successive output levels from 10 to 140.

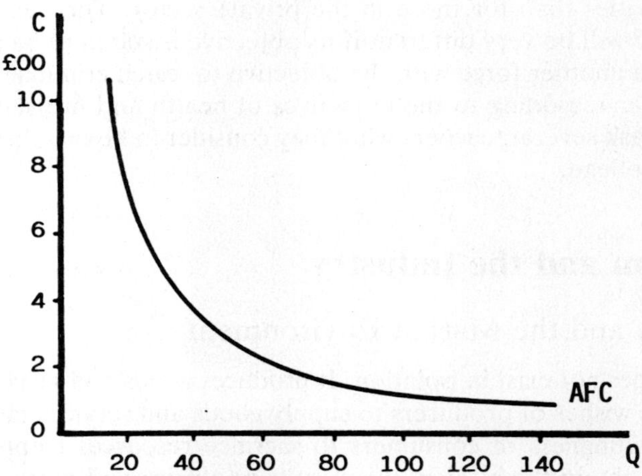

Fig. 4.1 The average fixed cost curve
The curve produced when a fixed cost of £1000 is divided by successive output levels from 10 to 140.

Note the steep fall as output rises up to around 60 to 80 units. Thereafter, the reduction in average cost is very small with each increment of output. This suggests that unless a firm is able to produce at least quantity level 60 it will not be able to enter the market with much hope of success. Above this output range, however, the cost reductions for increased output (assuming all firms face similar variable costs) are not very great.

We might say that around 80 to 90 units represents a **minimum efficient level of production**, a barrier that firms must surmount if they are to enter that particular market. In practice it is true, of course, that production levels are influenced by average total, rather than average fixed costs.

Nevertheless, in modern capital-intensive production the fixed costs are extremely important.

Number of producers supplying the market

If the minimum efficient level of production is high relative to total demand in the market then there can only be relatively few suppliers operating in the market. However, if it is low in relation to total market demand this does not necessarily mean that there will be a large number of suppliers because there may be other forces operating to keep the number small.

Other barriers

In addition to the barriers already noted, it is possible that the most successful firms deliberately manipulate market conditions in order to make entry difficult for potential competitors. Existing, established suppliers are likely to enjoy cost advantages in relation to new producers. This provides opportunities for establishing prices at levels designed to deter new entry while still providing satisfactory profits. Existing suppliers often market what is essentially the same product under **multiple brands** to give buyers the illusion of choice and competition and to make it difficult to establish a genuinely new product. Heavy advertising also increases costs for potential competitors and so helps to deter entry. Although sometimes illegal, market sharing may be practised. Markets may be shared among established producers by area of product. For these and other reasons total supply may be shared by very few producers even though the technical conditions of production might have been expected to favour a competitive market of small firms. It is technically possible to make washing detergents at low cost in the average school chemistry laboratory. Nevertheless the British market for these detergents is dominated by two very large firms. Clearly, there is more to the pattern of market supply than the costs of production. We must now start to examine the influences on supply a little more closely.

It is usual to use the term 'industry' to describe the group of firms supplying a particular class of product to a particular market area. Used in this wide sense 'industry' can be applied to manufacturing, distribution and to the supply of services. For statistical and other purposes, the Central Statistical Office prepares a classification of British industries called the Standard Industrial Classification. Other countries have similar official industrial classification systems.

Remember that a large firm may operate across several industries and supply to different markets in a number of different countries. Nevertheless, most do specialise in a fairly limited sector of production and even the largest normally have a 'dominant' interest in one industry or a small group of closely related industries.

Supply

Influences on Supply

Many textbooks explain how industry supply is made up from the aggregation of the output produced by all the firms operating in the industry. They then suggest that the supply or output curve for the individual firm can be deduced from its profit maximising conditions. In fact, as we show later in the book and in the computer exercises, this practice assumes that all firms seek to maximise profits and that they all operate in a particular form of market known as perfect competition. We have already argued that profit maximisation is only one of a number of possible objectives and we shall later argue that imperfect, rather than perfect forms of competition are normal in modern economies.

Our approach to supply in this book, therefore, is to suggest that total supply in an industry is the result of certain influences affecting the market as a whole and that the individual firms have to make their own decisions within the general market framework.

We now examine these influences. Remember that these will affect not only the firms actually supplying goods (for simplicity the term goods will be used to mean goods and/or services), but also those which have the productive facilities to produce the goods and could produce them if they so wished.

Price

Production is not an end in itself. Firms will make production decisions in an effort to achieve their **objectives**. You remember that there was some doubt about these objectives. However, in all the current theories either profit or revenue figure prominently. Both profit and revenue are directly dependent upon the price received for the goods. We shall assume that as the price rises, the quantity that firms are willing to supply will also rise. If price falls then quantity supplied also falls.

Factor costs

You should recall, now, the general production function introduced in Chapter 2. Remember this was:

$$Q = f(S,K,L,R)$$

or, if we include the level of technology (T);

$$Q = f(S,K,L,R,T)$$

By now you should readily identify the production factors denoted by the symbols inside the brackets (land, capital, labour and basic resources, technology). Total output is dependent on all these inputs and each firm is seeking to find the best combination of inputs in accordance with their prices and their relative efficiency in contributing to production.

Total supply to the market, therefore, will be influenced by the availability, the productivity and the price of the production factors. In general we assume that the quantity a firm is willing to supply will tend to rise if the factor prices fall or if the amount of production that can be achieved from a given input of factors rises. The converse will also apply.

Level of technology
This may be regarded as a separate input to production or as one of the most important influences on the strength of the relationship between inputs and output. As the level of technology rises and as more can be produced from any given 'bundle' of inputs, we would expect supply to rise.

Other production opportunities
Most firms have some choice of production from the resources and technical skills which they have available. If the conditions in one market become unfavourable they may be able to switch to another offering a better chance to achieve their objectives. A farmer, for example, may switch resources from dairy to meat production or between animals and arable farming according to changing market conditions. Prices of other products will, of course, influence other production opportunities.

Taxation
Whether or not a government is using taxation in a deliberate attempt to influence the volume or pattern of production, all taxes are likely to have some effect on business decisions. A more precise analysis is given in Chapter 7. You should recognise that tax changes may affect:

a **The price of goods** – for example, value added tax is imposed on producers but is added to prices charged to customers.
b **Factor prices** – for example, value added tax is imposed at all stages of production so that input prices are affected while the employers' share of national insurance 'contributions' and compulsory pension contributions may be regarded as a tax on the employment of labour.
c **Profits** – some taxes are imposed directly on the profits of business organisations; proprietors and partners in the personal sector pay taxes on profits as normal income; limited companies pay corporation tax based on company profits.

The Supply Curve

The above influences on supply can be represented in the form of the following general equation:

$$Q_s = f(P, C, T, O, t)$$

where:

Q_s = quantity of a good that firms are willing to supply to a market **in a given time period**
P = unit price of the good under consideration
C = factor costs
T = level of technology
O = other production opportunities, including the prices of other products
t = taxation

Economists normally regard the price of the product as the most important of the above influences and frequently wish to examine the price-quantity relationship with all the other influences assumed to be held constant. We can then say that:

$Q_s = f(P)$ with all other influences held constant

This relationship enables us to produce a supply schedule showing the quantities of a good that firms are willing to supply to a market at a given range of prices. Such a schedule can be represented graphically to form what is known as a supply curve. The following table and graph (Fig. 4.2) provide a simple illustration. Notice that quantity is always seen as a flow over a given time period. A change in price, all other influences remaining constant, results in a movement along the supply curve. For example, if price changes from £6 to £8 the quantity supplied will rise from 400 to 600 units.

Price £ per unit	*Q_s units per time period*
3	100
4	200
5	300
6	400
7	500
8	600
9	700

If there is a change in any of the other influences then the whole price-quantity schedule will change. This means a **shift in the whole supply curve**. For example, a change in the level of technology resulting in a reduction in inputs required to produce a given quantity of output would mean that at each price the firm would be prepared to supply more. For example, a quantity increase of 200 units at each price produces a shift in the curve as illustrated in Fig. 4.2b.

For general analytical purposes simple supply curves can be used with letter symbols replacing figures.

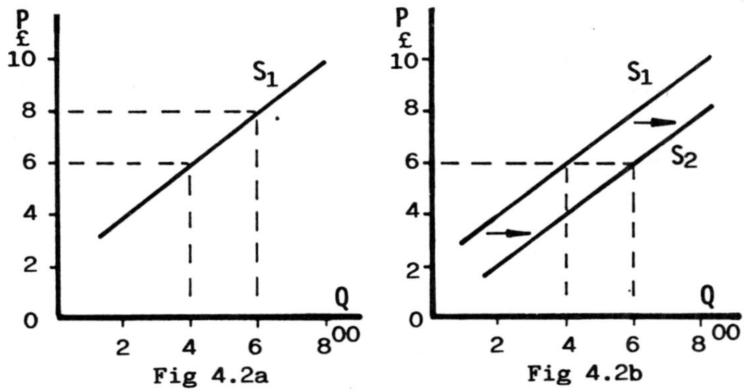

Fig. 4.2 The supply curve and a shift in the supply curve
Fig. 4.2a shows a movement along the curve with a price rise from £6 to £8 increasing quantity supplied from 400 to 600. Fig. 4.2b shows a movement in supply intentions so that at price £6 suppliers are willing to increase supply from 400 to 600.

Elasticity

It is not sufficient to know why supply changes. We need a precise and workable measure of these changes. To overcome the problem that any measure of the strength of an influence on quantity supplied is going to be concerned with two different units of measure we have to use ratios or proportional movements. We can then relate one ratio to another. When we relate the ratio of a quantity change or a proportional quantity change to that of the influence held to cause that change we have a measure which is termed **elasticity**. This measure is applied to the influences affecting both supply and demand. In this chapter we are concerned with supply.

Elasticity of Supply

Elasticity of supply, then, is the ratio of the proportional (or percentage) change in the quantity supplied of a product to a market to the proportional (or percentage) change in the influence causing that change. In practice, we need concern ourselves only with the effect of price changes so that:

The price elasticity of supply of a particular good (E_s) =

$$\frac{\text{the proportional (or \%) change in quantity supplied}}{\text{the proportional (or \%) change in its price}}$$

This can be stated in the form of:

$$\frac{\Delta Q}{Q} \div \frac{\Delta P}{P} \quad \text{or} \quad \frac{\Delta Q}{Q} \cdot \frac{P}{\Delta P} \quad \text{or} \quad \frac{P\Delta Q}{Q\Delta P}$$

where Δ (delta) is the symbol used to denote 'a change in' and where Q and P represent the quantities and prices of the goods under consideration.

It may now occur to you that we have a problem of measurement. Do we measure the proportional change from the starting quantities and prices or the finishing quantities and prices. Because we are concerned with proportions, the choice will affect the calculation, unless we are dealing with a precise **point** on the supply curve, in which case, if our mathematics is of a sufficient standard, we can simply use the differential calculus. The problem arises when we are concerned with a significant movement along the curve, i.e. an arc of the curve.

A better and more correct solution, and one gaining more general acceptance, is to use what is really the **arc elasticity of supply** by measuring around the midpoint of each change so that:

$$Q = \frac{(Q1 + Q2)}{2},\ P = \frac{(P1 + P2)}{2},\ \Delta Q = Q1 - Q2,\ \Delta P = P1 - P2$$

where Q1 and P1 are the quantities and prices before the change and Q2 and P2 are the quantities and prices after the change.

This practice enables us to produce the same figure for supply elasticity over a particular range of prices for both a price rise and a price reduction.

We can illustrate this by returning to the supply schedule where 400 units were supplied at the price of £6 and 500 units at £7.

$$\frac{100}{450} \div \frac{1}{6.5} = \frac{10}{45} \cdot \frac{65}{10} = 1.44$$

Calculate for yourself the values of point elasticity for a price rise of £1 at £6 and a price fall of £1 at £7.

To return to the calculation, however, if the result is greater than 1 we say that supply is price elastic; if it is less than 1, supply is said to be price inelastic; if just 1 then supply has unit elasticity. For quantity supplied we are assuming that the direction of the quantity movement is the same as that of the price movement – the supply curve has a positive slope – so the figure for price elasticity of supply is normally positive.

Supply Curves and Elasticity

It is very simple to see whether any particular supply curve is elastic, inelastic or if it has unit elasticity.

For linear curves, the following rules apply:

1 A curve which (when extended) passes through the point of origin has unit elasticity.
2 A curve which (when extended) passes through the vertical (price) axis is elastic.
3 A curve which (when extended) passes through the horizontal (quantity) axis is inelastic.

For non-linear curves the same rules apply to the tangent of a point on the curve which is under consideration. Note that the whole of the linear curve is elastic, inelastic or of unit elasticity. Contrast this later with the demand curve explained in Chapter 6.
A partial proof of these propositions, is given in a short appendix at the end of this chapter.

Supply, Elasticity and Time

The price elasticity of supply is measuring the extent to which producers are able to respond to a change in price. Such a reponse involves making production decisions in which the quantities and proportions of factors employed have to be changed and marketing and distribution arrangements altered. These changes take time and some producers are able to respond more quickly than others. However, all producers go through the same process of adjustment to change, though at different times. We can, therefore, suggest that the main influence on supply elasticity is time and that supply is likely to become more elastic as the time period lengthens.

This proposition is illustrated in Fig. 4.3 which shows how the supply curve shifts as the time period increases.

Exercises Relating to Chapter 4

1 By reference to the National Income 'Blue Book' or the equivalent in your country, chart the share of the public sector in Gross National Product over the past decade. Discuss:
a likely reasons for any trend evident from your chart;
b arguments for *either* an extension or a contraction of this share.
2 To what extent do the **objectives** of public sector enterprises differ from those of large corporate enterprises in the private sector?
3 Choose a well known consumer product. Identify and discuss the influences on:
a the supply
b price elasticity of supply, of that product using the analytical concepts provided by Chapter 4.
4 Obtain the published annual reports and accounts of three large public

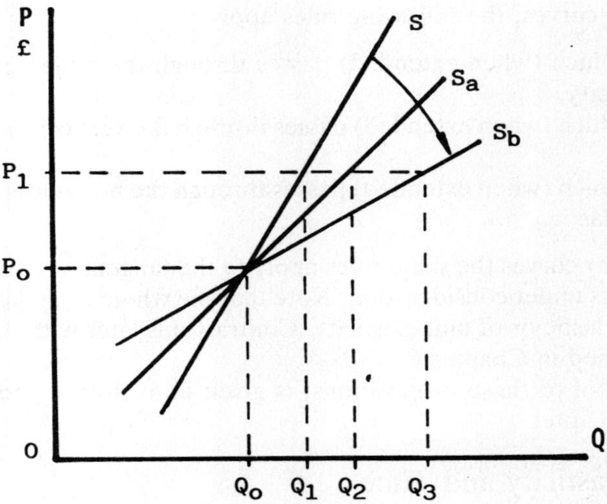

Fig. 4.3 Supply elasticity and time
In the very short term supply is highly inelastic. A rise in price P_0 to P_1 results in a small increase in quantity supplied to Q_1. In successive time periods producers are able to adjust production schedules and the supply curve shifts to S_a and then to S_b so that quantity supplied rises to Q_2 and Q_3 as supply becomes more elastic.

companies. On the evidence of these what do you consider to be the objectives of the companies?

Appendix: A Note on Supply Elasticity

Look carefully at Fig. 4.4 which shows a supply curve starting at the point of origin of the graph. Consider the effect of a change in price represented by ΔP. This produces a change in quantity represented by ΔQ. Now we can apply some basic geometry. Supply elasticity is:

$$\frac{\Delta Q}{Q} \div \frac{\Delta P}{P} = \frac{\Delta Q}{\Delta P} \cdot \frac{P}{Q}$$

but basic geometry tells us that:

$$\frac{P}{Q} = \tan\theta \text{ which also } = \tan\theta_1 \text{ which } = \frac{\Delta P}{\Delta Q} \text{ but}$$

$$\frac{\Delta Q}{\Delta P} = \frac{1}{\tan\theta} \text{ and } \tan\theta \cdot \frac{1}{\tan\theta} = 1$$

Therefore, from our definition of supply elasticity this must equal 1

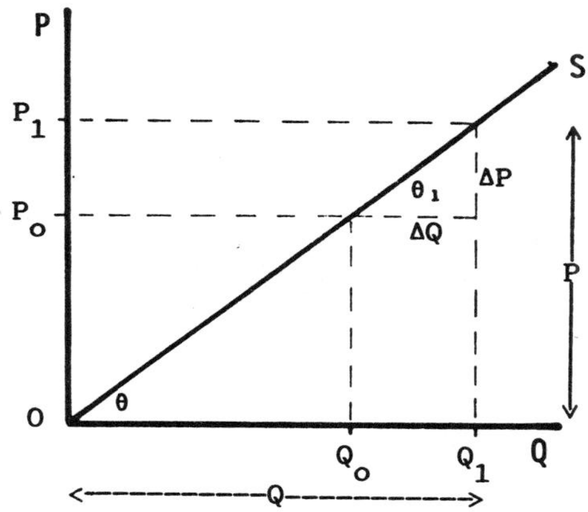

Fig. 4.4. A proof of unitary elasticity of supply
$P_1 - P_0 = \Delta P$ and $Q_1 - Q_0 = \Delta Q$

whatever the slope of the supply curve, when the curve passes through the point of origin of the graph.

You should now test your understanding by using the same technique to prove that a linear supply curve passing through the vertical (price) axis must be elastic and that one passing through the horizontal (quantity) axis must be inelastic.

You will find it helpful to extend the supply curve until it meets the negative side of the quantity axis in the first case and the negative side of the price axis in the second.

5

Utility and consumer demand

Utility

Meaning of Utility

So far we have seen how production uses factors to satisfy private and public wants. We now turn our attention to consumption and examine how people obtain satisfaction from consuming the goods and services that are produced.

Of course we can derive satisfaction from 'free goods', those obtained without any sacrifice of scarce resources. We cannot, indeed, survive without air to breathe. Our main interest as economists, however, lies in the choices made between competing uses for scarce resources so that it is the satisfaction derived from 'economic goods', those whose production does require a sacrifice of resources, that are of most concern to us. For reasons explained in Chapter 2 this satisfaction is called **utility** by economists. In Chapter 2 production was defined as the 'creation of utility'. This seems a simple enough idea but it is also the basis of much of what is called the theory of consumer demand.

Total and Marginal Utility

The measurement of utility has long presented problems. Attempts to give it a defined, absolute (also called cardinal) measure are clearly hazardous in view of the very great range and diversity of consumer wants. We can invent a measure of value, a 'util', say, but this has little real meaning. We can try to give it a money value but this becomes confused with price. What we can suggest, however, is that the amount of utility gained from any one purchase of a particular economic good depends on the amount of that good that we already possess. As we acquire more, the total utility from all our accumulated purchases of that good may still rise, but the amount of the increase resulting from each successive acquisition is likely to fall. Notice that we are looking at two aspects of utility.

a The **total utility** derived from a given quantity of a good.

b The **change in total utility** resulting from a change in the total quantity. This change in total utility is the **marginal utility** and we can, therefore, define marginal utility as **the change in total utility resulting from a very small, or unit, change in the quantity of an economic good consumed.** Mathematicians will recognise this as the first derivative of total utility with respect to quantity, i.e.:

$\frac{dU}{dQ}$ where U represents total utility and Q total quantity

The normal and reasonable assumption is that eventually, marginal utility will tend to diminish as more of the good is acquired. Ultimately, total utility will reach a maximum level. Beyond this, any further increases in quantity will reduce total utility. For example, every young family knows that it is uncomfortable to have a house but very little furniture. As time goes on more furniture is acquired and comfort increases. However, if there is a sudden acquisition of more furniture (from a relative, say) when the house is already full, this can be felt as a burden or nuisance and some furniture, that would have been welcomed at a lower level of possessions, may have to go.

The general assumptions relating to total and marginal utility, especially that of **diminishing marginal utility** just outlined, are shown graphically in Fig. 5.1 where the change in total utility as quantity rises is depicted in 'steps' along the curve.

Notice the diminishing size of the steps in total utility as quantity increases;

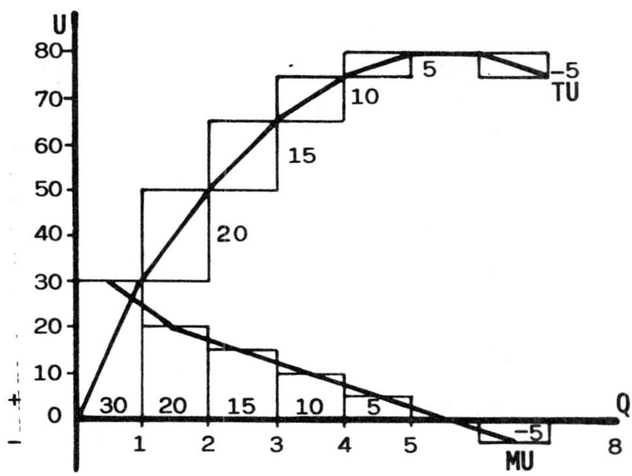

Fig. 5.1 Diminishing marginal utility
The diminishing steps in total utility are illustrated in the marginal utility curve.

for example, consumption of the first unit provides 30 units of utility, the second, 20, the third, 15 and so on. This shows clearly the idea of diminishing marginal utility.

The marginal utility curve represents the relationship between marginal utility and the same successive additions of quantity. This again brings out the negative relationship between quantity and marginal utility. For example, an increase from 3 to 4 units consumed adds 10 units of total utility but as quantity consumed rises to 5 the marginal utility falls to 5.

Utility and Price

If we now introduce money into our considerations, we can make some further observations. Money itself will have a utility because it can be used to purchase other goods. Any money I spend on good A is no longer available for spending on good B. Notice the concept of **opportunity cost** again. The rational consumer will spend some of his money to acquire an economic good as long as the additional utility gained from the purchase is more than the utility of the money spent. If we think in terms of buying one good or type of good then he or she will go on doing this up to the point where the two competing utilities are equal, i.e. where the marginal utility of the last unit of the good purchased equals the marginal utility of money multiplied by the number of money units needed to buy the good.

Putting this more formally we can say that the rational consumer is willing to purchase a single good(X) up to the quantity level where:

$$MU(X) = P(X) \cdot MU(money)$$

where:

MU(X)	=	Utility gained from buying the last unit of X
P(X)	=	Unit Price of the good X
MU(money)	=	the marginal utility of the last £ in money available for spending by the consumer
P(X)·MU(money)	=	the number of money units needed to buy X multiplied by the marginal utility of money, i.e. the utility obtained by spending money in the next most preferred way. This is the consumer's monetary valuation of the utility received from the marginal unit purchased of the good

When this stage is reached we can say that the consumer is in equilibrium because there is no further incentive for him to change his level of purchases. The two competing elements – money and the good(X) – have equal marginal values to him. This can also be expressed in the form:

$$\frac{MU(X)}{P(X)} = \frac{MU(money)}{P(money)}$$

where P(money) = the price of the money which = 1 (because it costs £1 to buy £1 worth of money).
Thus:

$$\frac{MU(X)}{P(X)} = MU(money) \qquad (A)$$

Normally, of course, there is a choice between differing goods and services as well as between goods and money. The problem facing the consumer, then, is to apportion the available money between the competing economic goods in such a way that the highest possible level of utility is achieved.

Once again, assuming rationality, the consumer will do this in such a way that the last pound (taking this as the relevant money unit) spent on each of the available goods will provide the same amount of additional utility. The **marginal utility per pound of spending** will now be the same for all goods purchased. If this is achieved there is again a state of equilibrium because no change in spending pattern can result in any increase in total utility. Total utility can **only** be increased by a change in spending pattern as long as it is possible to shift from one good to another whose marginal utility per pound of expenditure is higher. When all marginal utilities **per pound** are the same, this is no longer possible.

This equilibrium condition, taking into account the marginal utility of money, can be expressed formally as:

$$\frac{MU(X)}{P(X)} = \frac{MU(Y)}{P(Y)} = \ldots \frac{MU(money)}{P(money)}$$

As the P(money) = 1 then:

$$\frac{MU(X)}{P(X) \cdot MU(money)} = \frac{MU(Y)}{P(Y) \cdot MU(money)} = 1$$

Ideally, consumers would like to consume each good up to the point where its marginal utility is zero. This would maximise total utility. However, this is not possible. We can see why, because equation (A) above implies that the consumer's marginal utility of money would also be zero. Regrettably, most of us do not have incomes large enough for this happy state to be reached. Consequently, there is always likely to be an income (budget) constraint stopping us from consuming as much as we would wish of all goods.

Even when this constraint is operating it will still pay the consumer to seek that pattern of consumption where:

$$\frac{MU(X)}{P(X)} = \frac{MU(Y)}{P(Y)}$$

Notice that this is also:

$$\frac{MU(X)}{MU(Y)} = \frac{P(X)}{P(Y)}$$

which means that the ratio of the goods' marginal utilities is equal to the ratio of their unit prices.

Consider the following table of utilities for two goods X and Y whose prices are £5 and £6 respectively:

	X		*Y*	
Units purchased	*Total utility*	*Marginal utility*	*Total utility*	*Marginal utility*
0	0		0	
		50		80
1	50		80	
		40		50
2	90		130	
		30		40
3	120		170	
		25		36
4	145		**206**	
		20		30
5	**160**		236	

Suppose the consumer is buying 5X and 4Y. His marginal utility to price ratios for X and Y are:

$$\frac{MU(X)}{P(X)} = \frac{20}{5} = 4 \qquad \frac{MU(Y)}{P(Y)} = \frac{36}{6} = 6$$

The total utility from this mixture of X and Y is 160 from X + 206 from Y = 366.

The ratio of marginal utility to price is greater for Y than for X so our argument and the assumption of diminishing marginal utility suggest that consumers will benefit if they buy less of X and more of Y. Suppose they alter purchases to 4X + 5Y.

The ratios for this new package now become:

$$\text{for X} \quad \frac{25}{5} = 5 \qquad \text{for Y} \quad \frac{30}{6} = 5$$

Total utility from this changed mixture is now 145 from X + 236 from Y = 381 which represents an increase in utility of 15 achieved by spending an extra £1. If the consumers' budgets limit their total spending on X and Y to £50 this is the best they can achieve. The computer exercises in the utility section provide some simple calculations based on this principle.

The amount consumers purchase of any good will be determined by their budget constraints and by the valuation placed on other available goods. If we look again at the equilibrium condition:

$$MU(X) = P(X) \cdot MU(\text{money})$$

Then, assuming a constant marginal utility of money, it is possible to identify a clear relationship between price and the quantity demanded.

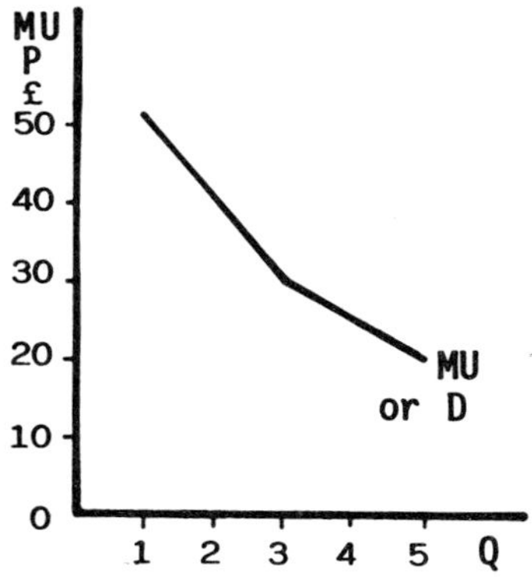

Fig. 5.2 The demand curve

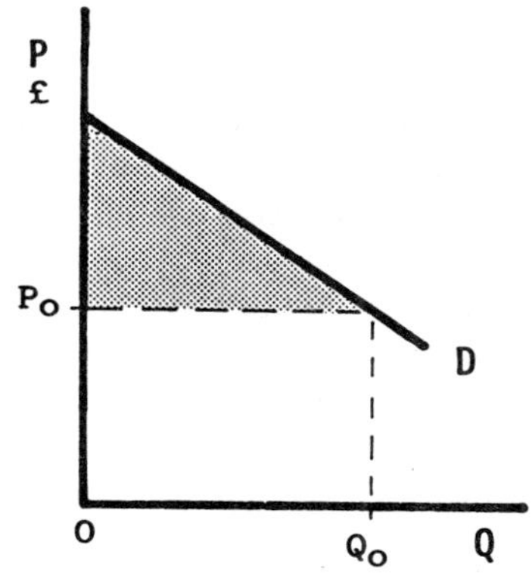

Fig. 5.3 The consumer surplus

This is shown in Fig. 5.2 which based on the utility of good X above. Assuming that MU = P · MU (money) the consumer is willing to pay £50 for the first unit, £40 for the second, £30 for the third and so on. This gives the normal price-quantity relationship of the demand curve in its usual form.

Consumer Surplus

The graph in Fig. 5.2 illustrates the fact that the consumer was prepared to pay £50 for the first unit but only £40 for the second and £30 for the third. This arises from the assumption of diminishing marginal utility. Normally, when we buy things we pay the same price for all units purchased. Thus, if the price is £30 we would be prepared to continue to buy as long as our valuation of the good is greater than or equal to the price. In this case we would buy three units because our valuation of the third unit = £30. Notice, however, that we would be able to buy the second unit for £10 less and the first unit for £20 less than we had been prepared to pay. This difference between what we would be prepared to pay for a good and the price we actually do pay is called the **consumer surplus**. In Fig. 5.3 the consumer surplus is represented by the shaded area between the line marking the market price and the demand curve.

The analysis of utility, so far, has provided us with some insights into demand but you may well have some questions about the assumptions that have been made. Are consumers always rational? This may seem doubtful but remember we have used rationality in a very limited sense here, largely to indicate only that consumers will seek to maximise utility. We have not questioned in any way the sense, desirability or social worth of the utility gained.

More serious is the implied assumption that has been made about the marginal utility of money. This has been regarded as remaining constant, no matter how much or how little we may have. A theory which suggests that all goods experience diminishing marginal utility, except the one good that enables us to acquire others, does contain an evident weakness. It would be better if we could eliminate the attempt to give utility an absolute value from our analysis.

If we abandon the attempt to give absolute or cardinal values for utility it is, nevertheless, still possible to assume ordinal values. By ordinal we mean that we can give goods an order of preference. We can say, for example, that we value Y more highly than X without actually placing any definite valuation on either Y or X. This is the assumption underlying the idea of the indifference curve.

Indifference Curves

General Features of Indifference Curves

A consumer indifference curve is a line on a graph showing combinations of goods or 'baskets' of goods which give the consumer the same total utility. An example is given in Fig. 5.4. The indifference curve I indicates that the consumer whose preferences are illustrated by this curve is equally satisfied by the following combinations of X and Y:

5Y + 2X; 2Y + 6X; or 1Y + 9X

Notice the change in relative values of X and Y suggested by the curve. When the consumer has only 1 unit of Y he is prepared to give up 3 units of X to gain a further unit of Y. However, when 4 units of Y are held, only 1 unit of X is sacrificed to gain a further unit of Y. Thus, at the low level of possession 1Y = 3X but at the higher level the marginal value of Y has diminished so that 1Y = 1X.

This principle is known as the **diminishing rate of marginal substitution**. If we accept it then we must also accept that indifference curves will always have the general shape indicated in Fig. 5.4, i.e. that they are convex to the graph's point of origin.

You may have already noticed the similarity between the idea of the indifference curve and that of the isoquant which features in Chapters 2 and 3. Indeed, if we use the same arguments as those of Chapter 3 we can show that the slope at any point of the indifference curve relating to two goods, X and Y, is equal to:

$$-\frac{MU(X)}{MU(Y)}$$

One curve illustrates one level of total utility. The further out from the origin the curve, the greater the level of utility achieved. We can envisage a series or 'map' of indifference curves showing the levels of possible total

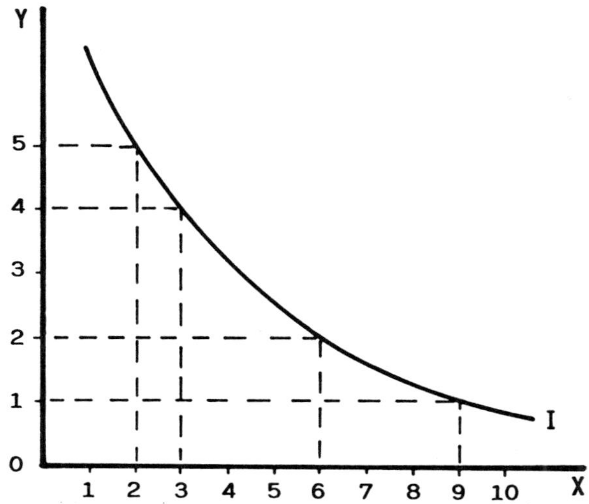

Fig. 5.4 The indifference curve
The consumer is equally satisfied by and, therefore, indifferent between any combination of **Y** and **X** represented by the curve **I**.

utility gained from various combinations of the goods available. A section of such an indifference map is shown in Fig. 5.5. The term **indifference curve** indicates that the consumer is indifferent to, or equally satisfied with, the different combinations of goods which it represents.

The Optimum Choice

In order to discover the best possible combination of goods open to the consumer we need to know:

a The unit price of each available good.
b The consumer income or budget, i.e. the total amount available for spending on the goods.

If we again assume two goods, the situation is illustrated in Fig. 5.6.

Suppose our budget is £36 and we can spend this on two goods X and Y. The unit prices are £3 for X and £2 for Y. In Fig. 5.6 AB is the line representing all the possible combinations of X and Y that can be obtained by spending £36 and assuming that each good is capable of being purchased in any fraction of a unit.

Notice that this line, which we call the **budget line** is similar to the isocost curve of Chapter 3. Again, using the arguments of that chapter we can

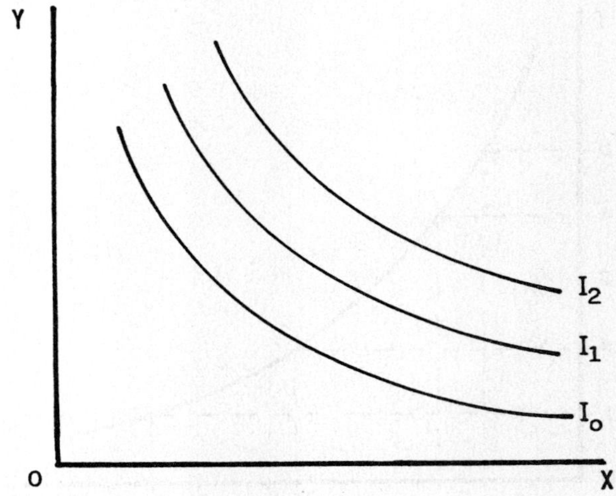

Fig. 5.5 Section of an indifference map
The three indifference curves represent three levels of total utility which increase with distance from the point of origin of the graph 0. I_2 represents greater total utility than I_1, which is greater than I_0.

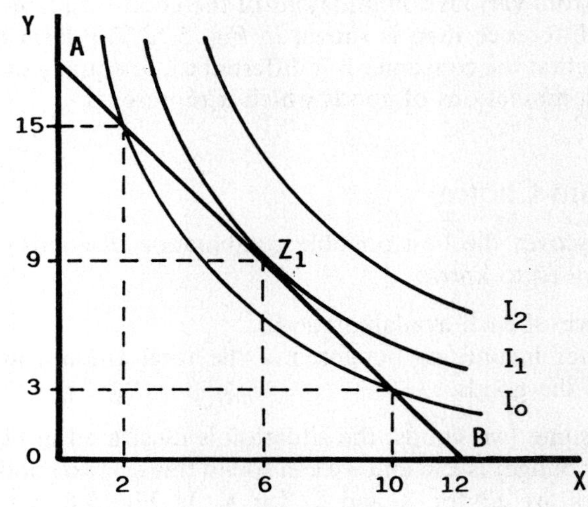

Fig. 5.6 The optimum choice
The best possible combination of **X** and **Y** given the budget line **AB** and the prices of **X** and **Y** is 6X + 9Y where the budget line touches the highest available indifference curve I_1.

show that the slope of the budget line is equal to:

$$\frac{-P(X)}{P(Y)}$$

where P(Y) = the price of Y and P(X) = the price of X.

Three levels of total utility are represented by I_0, I_1 and I_2. One gives a package of 10X + 3Y (£30 + £6) and the other gives 2X + 15Y (£6 + £30). Each of these packages is possible and each gives the same total utility of I_0, but is this the best the consumer can do?

Fig. 5.6 shows us that it is possible to reach a higher indifference curve, I_1. It just touches, i.e. is at a tangent to, this curve at point Z_1 which provides a package of 6X + 9Y (£18 + £18). No higher indifference curve – I_2 for instance – can be reached. Point Z_1 represents the best possible level of utility attainable under the given conditions and is the package that the rational consumer will choose.

When the budget line is tangential to an indifference curve their slopes will be the same. Thus:

$$\frac{MU(X)}{MU(Y)} = \frac{P(X)}{P(Y)}$$

This is similar to the argument of Chapter 3 that the best output level is where the slope of the isocost curve equals the slope of the isoquant. We can also make the deduction that the rational consumer, wishing to achieve the best purchasing pattern, will seek the mixture which produces:

$$\frac{MU(X)}{MU(Y)} = \frac{P(X)}{P(Y)} \text{ which is the same as: } \frac{MU(X)}{P(X)} = \frac{MU(Y)}{P(Y)}$$

Notice that this again brings us to the conclusion reached from the analysis of marginal utility, that the consumer will be in equilibrium and making the best possible use of his limited resources when the **ratio of the marginal utilities of available goods is equal to the ratio of their prices so that he obtains the same MU per £ spent on each.**

Indifference Curves and a Change in Income

If there is a change in the amount consumers can spend, without any change in the unit prices there will be a new budget line parallel to the old one.

In Fig. 5.7 it is assumed that the income available for spending has fallen from £36 to £24 but the unit prices of X and Y have stayed the same at £3 and £2 per unit. The new maximum possible purchase of X has thus fallen to 8 and that of Y to 12.

The resulting movement of the budget line brings it to a tangent at the

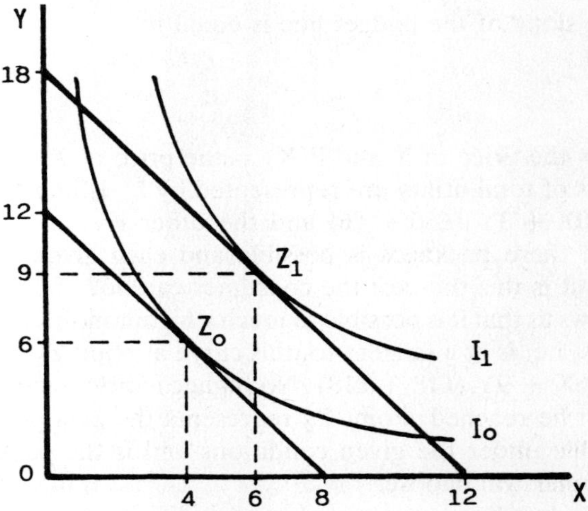

Fig. 5.7 The effect of an income change
A lower income produces a new budget line which can only reach the lower indifference curve I_0.

new and lower indifference curve I_0 where the new chosen package is made up of 6Y + 4X (£12 + £12) at point Z_0.

The Effect of a Price Change

We can also use indifference curves to illustrate the effect of a price change. This is shown in Fig. 5.8 where the lowest indifference curve I has been discarded and a second budget line AC, has been introduced to show the effect of a reduction in the unit price of X to £2.25. The maximum possible purchases of X (no Y purchased) rises from 12 (£36 ÷ 3) to 16 (£36 ÷ 2.25). This change in price brings the new budget line, AC to a tangent at Z_2 to the higher indifference curve I_2. The new package is made up of 6.75Y + 10X. The change in price has resulted in an increase in purchases of X, whose price has fallen, and a fall in purchases of Y, whose price has stayed the same.

Indifference Curves and Demand Curves

Indifference curves can help us to deduce the shape of demand curves which show the price-quantity relationship for particular goods.

Look again at Fig. 5.8 and consider what happens to good X. At a price of £3 the quantity consumed, indicated by the point Z_1, was 6 units. When the price fell to £2.25 the quantity consumed rose to 10 units. This change is illustrated by the graph of Fig. 5.8b where quantity is measured on the horizontal axis and price on the vertical axis.

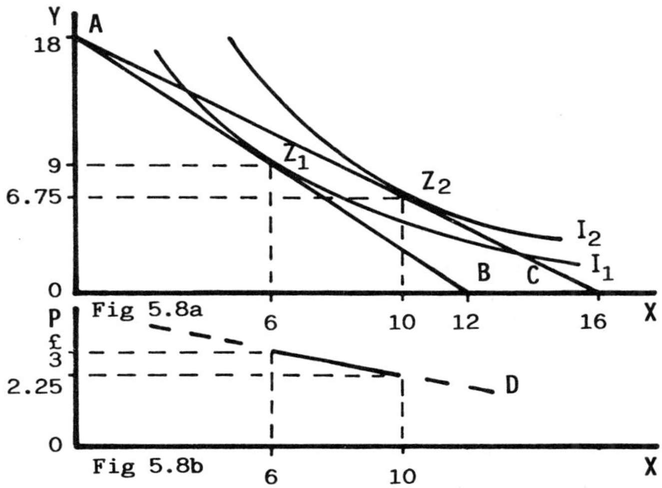

Fig. 5.8 Indifference curves and the demand curve
When the unit price of **X** falls the preferred consumption of **X** rises from 6 to 10 units. This suggests the price-quantity relationship indicated by the demand curve **D**.

Of course, this records quantities for two price levels only and we would need rather more for realistic demand estimation. Nevertheless, if we have reason to believe that the demand for X is linear over a limited price range we can deduce the quantities likely to be demanded between and, perhaps, a little beyond the two known prices. This is suggested by the dotted line extensions.

The Income and Substitution Effect of a Price Change

Look once more at Fig. 5.8 where the shift in the budget line enabled the consumer to move from the package of Z_1 to Z_2 and gain the increased quantity of goods at the new level of total utility. Concentrate on the change in consumption of X the price of which fell. The increased quantity of X is partly the result of the changed ratio of marginal utilities to prices caused by the price reduction. This is called the **substitution effect**. It is also partly the result of the increase in spending power brought about by the price fall. For example, suppose I have to buy 50 litres of petrol per week to travel to work. If the price of petrol falls by 10p per litre then I have an extra £5 per week to spend. I may choose to spend some of this extra money on more petrol for pleasure driving. Because my real spendable income has increased this is called the **income effect**.

We can identify these effects in Fig. 5.9 where the original equilibrium position, before any price change, is at A. After the price change the new equilibrium is at B.

Imagine that, after the change in price of X, the consumer's income was reduced to such an extent that he was brought back to the original utility indifference curve, I_0, thus removing the income effect of the price change. We can do this by drawing what is known as an **income compensation budget line** parallel to the new budget line but just touching the original indifference curve I_0 at C. At this point on the indifference curve X_c units of X would be bought. This indicates that $X_c - X_a$ is the amount of increase that can be attributed to the substitution effect, i.e. by the **movement along the indifference curve resulting from the relative price change**. The remainder of the increased consumption of X, $X_b - X_c$ units, can be attributed to the **shift to a higher level of total utility** – the income effect.

Notice that in this illustration there is also a small income effect on the consumption of Y, the demand for which rises slightly. This is not unusual. If the price of petrol falls, for example, I may decide to spend some of my extra income on other preferred purchases.

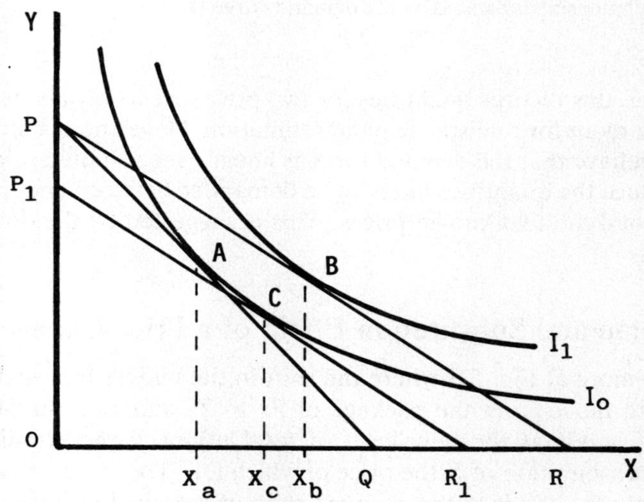

Fig. 5.9 The normal income and substitution effect
A price reduction for **X** shifts the budget line from **PQ** to **PR** allowing the consumer to move from **A** on indifference curve $\mathbf{I_0}$ to **B** on the higher indifference curve $\mathbf{I_1}$. A compensating reduction in income represented by the line $\mathbf{P_1R_1}$ shows a movement along the original indifference curve to **C** caused by the change in relative prices of **X** and **Y**. **A** to **C** is the substitution effect. **C** to **B** on the higher indifference curve is the income effect.

Must the substitution and income effects always be the same? Will the combined effects of income and substitution always lead to quantity changes that are the reverse of price changes? Look now at Fig. 5.10. In this illustration the original equilibrium package is again at A and the new equilibrium, following the price fall of X, is again at B. The substitution effect resulting from the movement along the original indifference curve, I_0, is at X_c but now the income effect produces a **fall** in quantity desired. Quantity X_b is at a lower level than X_c though it is still higher than the original quantity, X_a. Whenever, as in this case, the final equilibrium lies between the original quantity (X_a) and the increase attributable to the changed price ratios (the substitution effect of $X_c - X_a$) the good is described as **inferior**. This is because the rise in real spendable income leads to a fall in quantity consumed. This tendency, which is linked with a desire to switch preferences to goods which the consumer can now afford at the higher income is examined further in Chapter 6.

Now consider Figure 5.11. Once more the original budget line gives an equilibrium package of A, and the original quantity of X required is X_a. The price of X falls and the consumer moves to the higher indifference curve I_1 and the new equilibrium package of B. Now, however, the quantity required **falls** to X_b. The substitution effect, ($X_c - X_a$) however,

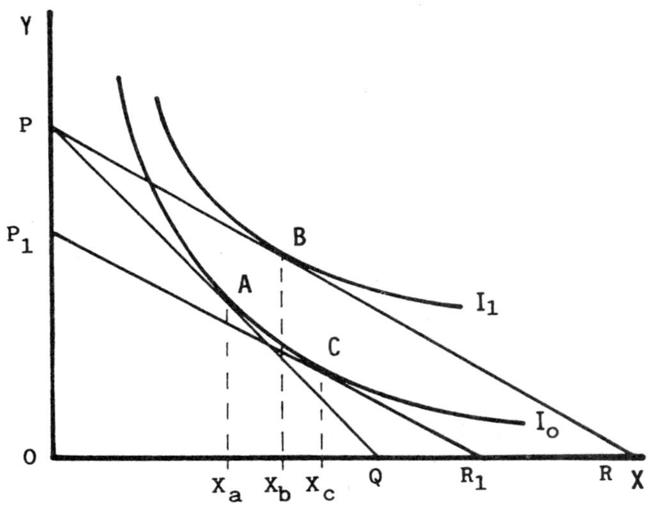

Fig. 5.10 The income and substitution effect for an inferior good
The price change and income compensation are the same as in Fig. 5.9. Here, however, the income effect of moving to **B** on the higher indifference curve I_1 is to reduce consumption of **X** from X_c to X_b. A good whose consumption falls as income rises is said to be inferior.

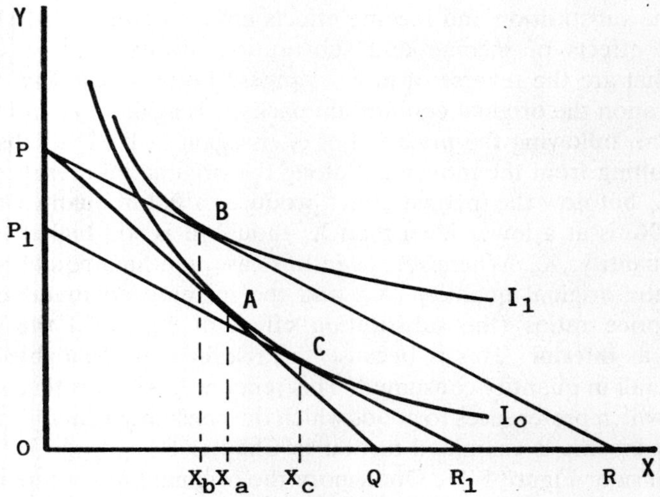

Fig. 5.11 Income and substitution effect for a Giffen good
The price change and compensation of income are the same as those in Fig. 5.10. Here, however, the reduction from income effect is so great that it outweighs the increase resulting from the substitution effect and consumption falls as the result of the fall in price. For such a (rare) Giffen good a rise in price would also lead to a rise in consumption.

is still positive, but is outweighed by the very strong income effect $X_c - X_b$. Such a good would be described as a **Giffen good** and this (very rare) case of a price fall leading to a fall in quantity consumed is also discussed further in Chapter 6.

Notice, however, that although the income effect may lead to a positive or a negative change in quantity consumed, the substitution effect is **always negative**. It always tends to change the quantity consumed in the reverse direction from that of the price movement.

Exercises Relating to Chapter 5

1 Complete the following table:

Units purchased	*Product A Total utility*	*Marginal utility*	*Product B Total utility*	*Marginal utility*
1	100		80	
		60		50
2	160			
				40
3	210		170	
		45		
4			195	
				15
5	295			

a What combination of A and B would a rational consumer buy if the unit price of A is £9 and of B is £5 and the total budget available for spending on the two products is £60?

b What would be the effect of a reduction in the unit price of A to £8 all other conditions remaining unaltered?

Justify your answers using the analytical concepts explained in Chapter 5.

2 With your own figures and the help of graph paper, construct a demand curve using simple indifference curve analysis.

3 In Great Britain between 1955 and 1965, incomes rose but the quantity demanded of motorcycles fell. How do you explain this? Illustrate and discuss this effect with the help of indifference curves.

4 Discuss and illustrate the income and substitution effects of price changes. Why are these important to governments when they change expenditure taxes.

6

Demand

The Influences on Demand

Utility analysis has suggested three major influences on the demand for a product. Chapter 5 showed how the demand for both X and Y could change following a change in the price of X, thus suggesting that demand for a product could be influenced both by changes in its own price and in the prices of other goods. Chapter 5 also showed how changes in spendable or disposable income could affect demand. These and other influences on demand require further examination. Up to this point we have referred to consumers and the consumer without distinguishing between the two terms.

Some textbooks point out that total demand in a market is the sum of the actions of all the individual buyers, that market demand is the aggregate of individual demand preferences. Mathematically this, of course, is correct but it is not very helpful to practical economists who require to work with higher degrees of probability than can be provided by the whims and fancies of individuals. It is not possible to derive market demand curves by identifying and aggregating the wishes of individuals. It is, however, both possible and put into common practice to identify and record the actions of groups. A supermarket manager cannot point to individual customers and predict accurately what each will purchase. He can and does predict the average amount that each 1000 customers passing through the store will spend and he can apportion their spending between categories of goods with some confidence. Actual demand functions on the basis of which firms have to make production and marketing decisions are derived from the study of identifiable market groups. It is with demand in this sense that we are now concerned.

The Good's Own Price and the Prices of Other Goods

We have already shown from a theoretical foundation how a demand curve can be derived and how this demand curve suggests that the quantity demanded of a good moves in the opposite direction from its price. This reflects the normal relationship, of which there is ample practical evidence, between price and quantity.

The effect of other price changes will depend on the relationship between the goods under consideration.

If the goods are **substitutes** for each other and if consumers are willing to buy more of one to compensate for less of the other then we can expect a rise in price of one to produce a rise in demand for the other. There is a positive relationship between quantity purchased of A and the price of B when A and B are substitutes. Beef and lamb are common examples of this relationship.

If the goods are **complements** and, therefore, related in that the utility derived from one depends at least in part, on the availability of the other then a change in price of one will have a similar effect to a change in price of the other. For example, most people tend to take photographs when they are on holiday. If the price of foreign holidays falls and more people go on 'package tours' the demand for camera film can be expected to rise.

It is not always necessary for there to be any direct connection between goods for a price change of one to influence demand for the other. If a good is a major element in regular household spending a rise in its price will reduce the income available for spending on other goods. If the price of petrol rises, many people will not find it possible to reduce the amount of petrol they buy immediately. It takes time to adjust spending and living patterns, to replace a car with a smaller one or to live closer to work. During this period of re-adjustment the demand for goods not considered essential for normal daily life is likely to fall, though these have no links with petrol and motoring.

Income

Normally we expect a rise in income to lead to a rise in demand for most goods. To have any effect, however, the income affected must be that part which is available for spending on the goods under examination. It is always with the net income that remains after payment of taxes and 'semi-taxes' such as national insurance and compulsory pension contributions, that we are concerned. Even part of this net income is not truly disposable once a particular life pattern has been adopted. Most households have to pay mortgage interest or rent and other regular household bills such as those for fuel and transport between home and work. The amount of income (if any) remaining after these payments have been made is called **discretionary income**. A change in house mortgage interest can make a significant change in the level of household discretionary income and thus influence the demand for a wide range of goods.

Although the normal expectation is for demand to move in the same direction as income changes there are exceptions as was shown in Chapter

5. When incomes in the UK were rising in the 1950s and 1960s demand for motorcycles fell as people changed to motorcars as preferred forms of personal transport. Motorcycles could, then, be defined as **inferior goods** in comparison with cars. You should make a list of other examples and discuss these with your teacher. This can be an important aspect of changing demand in a developing country.

Consumer Taste

We all know that fashions change, sometimes quickly, as for skateboards, sometimes slowly, as for breakfast foods. Some changes such as those towards less formal clothes and away from tobacco smoking, reflect deep movements in social attitudes and lifestyles. Others may simply reflect passing fashions. Firms have to be aware of these changes however difficult they may be to predict and to measure.

Business Marketing and Advertising

Many business managers and economists would argue that the firm does not exist just to satisfy consumer wants and to adapt to changes in taste. It also stimulates and develops these wants. One path to business success lies through the ability to detect latent desires and trends and then, by producing suitable goods and by vigorous marketing, to turn these into actual demand.

At this stage we can simplify our analysis by recognising that demand will be influenced by advertising. For goods which face competition from substitutes in established markets demand will depend not so much on the absolute volume of advertising but on changes in advertising in relation to the advertising of competitors. If firm A increases its advertising by, say 25% and competitors do not make any change, then we would expect firm A to achieve some increase in sales.

Size of the Potential Market

Total demand achieved must also depend on the number of possible customers. This is affected partly by decisions of the firm and partly by external influences. The two may, of course, be related. For example, a firm may decide to extend its marketing operations from Europe into Asia. This decision may be taken in the light of an extension of television networks into some large Asian cities allowing the firm to make wider use of advertising film. Changes in communications, including transport networks, have always been important in determining market size.

On the other hand some changes may appear to be quite outside the firm's influence. Changes in population structure caused by rising or falling birth and death rates will affect total potential markets for a wide range of household and family goods and services.

Expectations of the Future

A person's decision to buy – or not to buy – now, depends partly on his or her reaction to the variables outlined above, and also to expectations concerning their future movements. I may decide to buy a car this week even if its price has just risen, if I believe that the price may be higher still next month. If I am making the purchase with the help of a credit arrangement involving regular future payments I shall be more ready to buy if I believe that my income is likely to rise in the coming months. I shall be less inclined to buy if I believe that prices may fall or fear that my employer is likely to be making workers redundant in the near future.

Other Influences

The above are the main influences considered to determine demand. There are, of course, others. For example, if the quality or reliability of a domestic appliance, such as a dishwashing machine, improves then more people will want to use it.

Changes in Demand

The Demand Equation

We can summarise the main influences in the form of the following general equation, which applies to a single time period. If we wish to examine demand over different periods of time then this variable would also have to be taken into account.

$$Q_d = f(P, P_0, Y, T, A, N, E, \ldots Z)$$

In this equation:

Q_d = the quantity demanded of a good within an identifiable market
P = the good's own price
P_0 = the prices of other goods
Y = disposable income
T = taste
A = advertising or marketing effort
N = the size of the potential market
E = expectations of the future
Z = other influences not specifically identified, e.g. changes in time period or in weather

The function f( ) indicates that the quantity demanded depends upon the influences denoted within the brackets but we do not want to specify the exact form that the relationship is likely to take in each case. One possible relationship could take the form:

$$Q = a{\cdot}P + b{\cdot}P_0 + c{\cdot}Y + d{\cdot}T + g{\cdot}A + m{\cdot}N + p{\cdot}E$$

It can be argued that the expressions N and E can be omitted from the equation on the grounds that these influence the values of a, b, c, and d. Mathematically, this is the more desirable procedure but, at this stage, adding them to the equation helps to emphasise their importance.

Setting out a demand equation in this way also helps to remind us that these various influences can, at the same time, be pulling in different directions. Prices may be falling, but so may incomes and expectations of future incomes may be gloomy. The total effect may be to reduce quantities demanded even though this does not contradict the general tendency for people to buy more at lower than at higher prices. The total change in quantity demanded is thus the consequence of **all** the influences.

This type of relationship shows quite clearly that there are a large number of influences on the quantities of goods that are bought. In order that we may gain a thorough understanding of the way market prices are determined we initially change one variable at a time while holding the others constant. Once we clearly understand how each variable can influence the quantity demanded, we can change two or three at once. The microcomputer helps us to do this easily.

Demand Curves

As with supply curves the major influence used to produce the demand curve is the good's own price. Assuming that all other influences remain constant (sometimes known as the *ceteris paribus* rule), we can produce a schedule of quantities demanded at a range of prices and represent this in a normal graph.

Fig. 6.1 is the demand curve derived from the simple table or demand schedule shown. Here a change in price from £5 to £6 results in a movement along the demand curve and a change in quantity demanded from 700 to 600 units per time period.

P (£ per unit)	*Q (Units per time period)*
3	900
4	800
5	700
6	600
7	500
8	400

A change in any of the other influences, such as income, prices of other goods, taste and so on is illustrated by a shift in the whole demand curve,

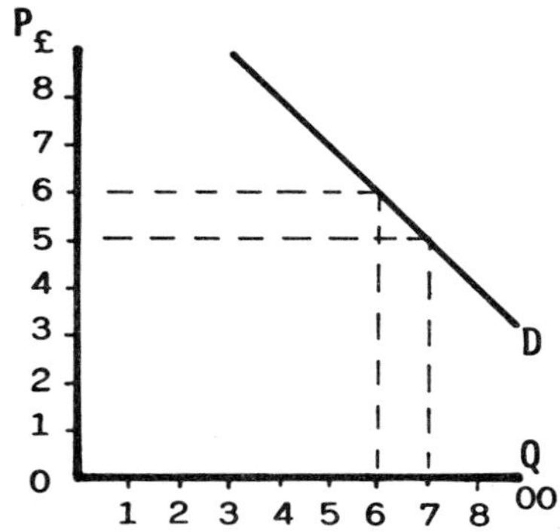

Fig. 6.1 The demand curve
This shows the normal price-quantity relationship. The price change results in a movement along the curve.

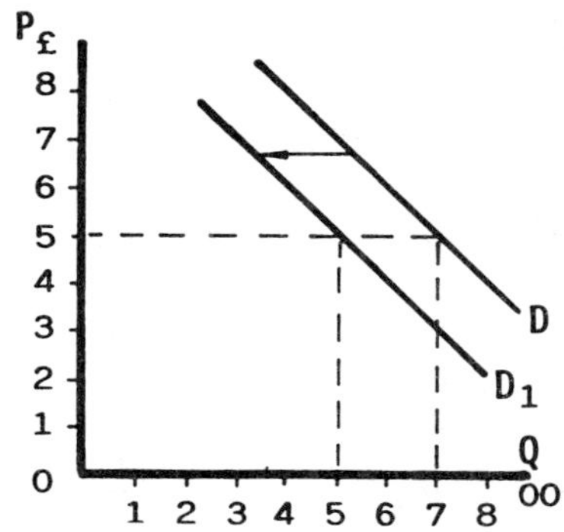

Fig. 6.2 A shift in the whole demand curve
The curve shifts **D** to D_1 and the quantity consumers wish to buy as each price falls.

i.e. in a new schedule of quantities demanded at each price within the range. Such a change is illustrated in Fig. 6.2 where a movement of the curve from D to D_1 results in a fall in the quantity consumers are willing to buy at each price. For example, at a price of £5 per unit quantity demanded falls from 700 to 500 units per time period.

The Giffen Effect

The idea of the Giffen effect was introduced in Chapter 5. It has been suggested, notably by Giffen, that there could be exceptions to this general rule. Giffen observed that in Ireland during years of deep depression and hardship, the demand for potatoes rose as their price increased. He argued that the rising prices forced people to forgo higher level foods and concentrated demand on the staple diet of the time – potatoes. From time to time people have pointed to other examples of the so-called 'Giffen' price-quantity relationship. It is said, for instance, that people will often buy more tomatoes at higher than at lower prices and demand for places at the more expensive private (public) schools is usually higher than at the less expensive establishments. There is, however, some doubt as to whether such examples are genuine 'Giffen' goods. Different grades of product might more accurately be regarded as different goods with separate demand curves.

Elasticities of Demand

Having identified the various influences on demand, we need some precise tools of measurement so that we can measure the effect of a change in one or more of the separate variables. This measure is provided by the concept of elasticity. This is the responsiveness of demand to changes in the influences which affect it. It is:

$$\frac{\text{the proportional (or \%) change in quantity demanded}}{\text{the proportional (or \%) change in a determining variable}}$$

Price Elasticity of Demand

If we apply this to what is recognised as one of the most important of the variables, the good's own price, we have the **price elasticity of demand**. Relating the proportional changes to the actual prices and quantities and using the symbol E_d for price elasticity of demand we can make the statement:

$$E_d = \frac{\Delta Q}{Q} \div \frac{\Delta P}{P} \text{ which } = \frac{\Delta Q}{\Delta P} \cdot \frac{P}{Q} \text{ where } \Delta = \text{a change in} \ldots$$

Because a price increase normally leads to a fall in the quantity demanded, and vice versa, most goods have a negative price elasticity of demand. In the calculations, either the price or quantity change, whichever is falling, should be preceded by the negative sign. The elasticity value should also carry the negative sign.

It may now occur to you that if we make the calculations for a price increase we shall obtain a different answer than for a price decrease over the same price and quantity range. This is because the proportions will be based on different initial price and quantity levels. To overcome this problem, the figures for Q and P can be found by taking the midpoint of the change. This means that:

$$Q = \frac{Q_1 + Q_2}{2} \text{ and } P = \frac{P_1 + P_2}{2}$$

where Q_1 and P_1 are the quantity and price levels before the change and Q_2 and P_2 are the quantity and price levels after the change. For example, the price of X rises from £2 to £3 and as a direct consequence the quantity demanded of X falls from 60 to 40 units per week.
Here $P_1 = 2$, $P_2 = 3$, so $P = 2.50$
and $Q_1 = 60$, $Q_2 = 40$, so $Q = 50$ so that:

$$E_d = \frac{-20}{50} \div \frac{1}{2.5} \text{ which } = \frac{-2}{5} \cdot \frac{2.5}{1} \text{ which } = -1$$

Calculations made in this way are usually referred to as **arc elasticity**. Calculations using proportions of the original quantities and prices are known as **point elasticity**.

Point calculations are made when we wish to calculate the elasticity at a particular price, i.e. at a definite point on the demand curve. Arc elasticity should always be used when we wish to calculate the effect of a movement in price, i.e. a movement along the demand curve.

In the following explanations where the numbers referred to are negative, we actually consider the corresponding positive number (mathematicians will recognise this as the modulus).

In the above example, and looked at in this way, the proportional changes are the same and we can say that the price elasticity of demand is unity or that there is unitary price elasticity of demand. When the proportional change in quantity is greater than one and then demand is said to be **price elastic**. A result less than one, indicating that the proportional change in quantity is less than that of price is said to show that demand is **price inelastic**.

Although we have used the modulus of the relevant numbers in the above explanation we still say that the price elasticity of demand is negative.

A further feature of price elasticity of demand is that in most cases, and always when the demand curve is linear (a straight line), elasticity changes as price changes. Normally we expect demand to become more elastic as the price rises. Common sense supports this view; as price increases we become more price conscious. This is illustrated in Fig. 6.3, where at A on the demand curve demand is price elastic, at B elasticity is at unity and at C demand has become price inelastic.

An interesting example of an exception to this normal expectation is where the proportional change in quantity demanded remains the same as the proportional change in price at all prices within a given range, i.e. demand has a price elasticity of unity over this range. This produces the curve of $P \times Q = a$ where a is constant. This is illustrated in Fig. 6.4, where the product of price and quantity is £24 at each point on the curve. Mathematicians will recognise this as the rectangular hyperbola. We would not expect this condition to hold over a large price range or over a long period of time but it is found for a number of goods over a limited price range. For example, a family which habitually pays the same amount for the weekend joint of meat in spite of changes in its price is showing unit elasticity of demand.

We have seen that, apart from some special cases, price elasticity of demand is likely to vary with the price of the good. It increases as price increases. There are some other influences. One is the price in relation to income. We are likely to be less concerned with a change in price of an article which represents only a very small proportion of weekly income than with a change affecting a major household item costing the equivalent of several month's income. We might still buy the high priced item but could, perhaps, delay the purchase for several months and this would have a significant influence on demand. Attempts have been made to distinguish between 'necessities' with low price elasticity and 'luxuries' with high price

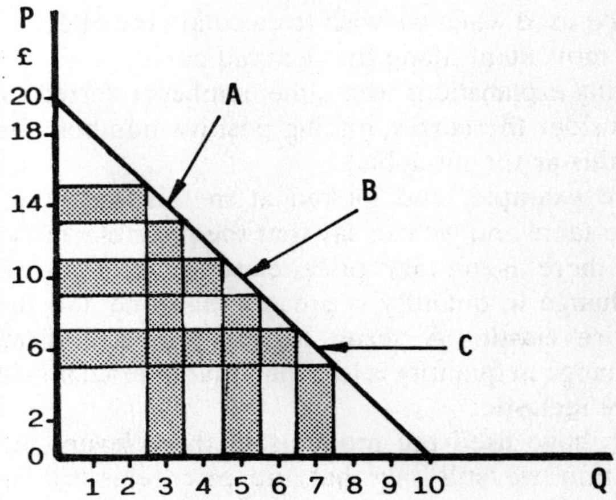

Fig. 6.3 Price elasticity of demand and the linear demand curve.

At **A** $E_d = \frac{-1}{3} \div \frac{2}{14} = \frac{-7}{3} = -2.33$ $E_d > 1$ (elastic)

At **B** $E_d = \frac{-1}{5} \div \frac{2}{10} = \frac{-5}{5} = -1$ $E_d = 1$ (unity)

At **C** $E_d = \frac{-1}{7} \div \frac{2}{6} = \frac{-3}{7} = -0.44$ $E_d < 1$ (inelastic)

At **A** the proportional change in quantity is greater than the proportional change in price. At **C** the reverse is the case while at **B** the proportional changes are the same.

elasticity of demand. But some writers, including Lispey, have shown that there is little practical justification for this.

We should also be careful to identify precisely the nature of the product in relation to elasticity. Washing powder, for example, has a low price elasticity of demand, but X's 'special dazzle' powder may be more price elastic because there are ready substitutes. The availability of substitutes is likely to be one of the most important influences on the price elasticity of demand.

Cross Elasticity of Demand

Another elasticity which is relevant to demand is called the cross elasticity of demand E_x. This measures the proportional change in the quantity demanded of one good in relation to the proportional change in the price of another. This can be expressed in the form:

$$E_x\,A,B = \frac{\Delta Q_A}{Q_A} \div \frac{\Delta P_B}{P_B}$$

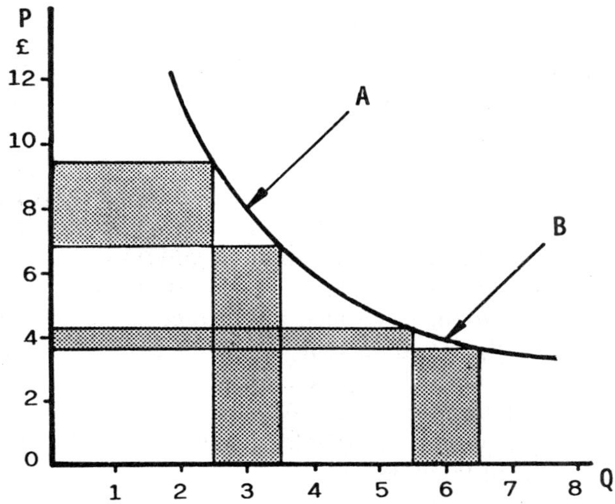

Fig. 6.4 The demand curve with constant unitary price elasticity

At **A** $E_d = \frac{-1}{3} \div \frac{2.67}{8} = -1$ and total revenue = £24

At **B** $E_d = \frac{-1}{6} \div \frac{0.67}{4} = -1$ and total revenue = £24

The proportional change in price = the proportional change in quantity at all points on the curve which is the graph of **P** × **Q** = 24.

A little mathematical manipulation produces the following rearrangement:

$$E_x\ A,B = \frac{P_B}{Q_A} \cdot \frac{\Delta Q_A}{\Delta P_B}$$

The calculations should be based on the midpoints of change and thus represent a form of arc elasticity.

Cross elasticity of demand will be positive (+) or negative (−) depending upon the relationship between the two goods. If they are substitutes then a rise in the price of A will produce a rise in demand for B and E_x will be positive. If the goods are complementary to each other (foreign holidays and camera film), the price rise can be expected to produce a quantity fall so that E_x will be negative as for price elasticity of demand. The closer the degree of substitutability or complementarity the higher is likely to be the value of cross elasticity of demand.

Income Elasticity of Demand

Following the same procedures we can produce income elasticity of demand to measure the effects of a change in net, disposable income, symbol E_y.

$$E_y = \frac{\Delta Q}{Q} \div \frac{\Delta Y}{Y} \text{ and this } = \frac{\Delta Q}{\Delta Y} \cdot \frac{Y}{Q}$$

For most goods we would expect a rise in income to produce an increase in demand, giving a positive result for E_y. Such goods are usually termed 'normal'. For inferior goods as defined in Chapter 5, income elasticity of demand would carry the negative sign. Arc elasticity calculations should again be used. The more highly priced goods and those associated with rising living standards are likely to have the higher income elasticities. These would include major household durables such as freezers and services such as foreign holidays.

The terms inelastic, elastic and unitary are applied to income and cross elasticities for values that are less than one, more than one or unity.

Examples of actual estimates of price, cross and income elasticities relating to some broad food groups are contained in the exercises which follow.

Exercises Relating to Chapter 6

1 *a* Identify and discuss the relative importance of the various influences affecting the demand for home computers.
  b What problems are there in defining the market for home computers?
  c Bearing in mind that a computer requires software, what problems are there in identifying the 'price' of a home computer?

2 Discuss the view that there is no such thing as a Giffen good.

3 Below is a table of the National Food Survey Committee's estimates of the price elasticities of demand for certain broad food groups for two periods, 1967–74 and 1973–80.

	1967–1974	**1973–1980**
Milk and cream	−0.16	−0.09
Carcase meat	−0.60	−1.23
Other meat	−0.95	−1.14
Fish	−0.92	−1.09
Eggs	−0.11	−0.12
Potatoes	−0.18	−0.18
Fresh fruit	−0.57	−0.75
Bread	−0.09	−0.56
Beverages	−0.63	−0.43

a What do you consider to be the main features of these figures?

b Assuming that the figures are reasonably accurate, what explanations would you offer for the differences or lack of differences between the two periods?

c Using the 1973–1980 column, calculate the effect on quantity sold of a 10% increase in the prices of carcase meat, fish, eggs and milk, all other things remaining unchanged.

4 The following exercises relate to the table of the National Food Survey Committee's estimates of certain cross-price elasticities for the period 1973–1980.

a Comment on the figures and identify the apparent complements and substitutes.

b Calculate the effect of 20% price rises for carcase meat on the demand for fish and for milk on the demand for bread.

Cross elasticities of demand

Carcase meat	Other meat	0.58
Other meat	Carcase meat	0.51
Fish	Carcase meat	0.51
Eggs	Bread	−0.13
Sugar and preserves	Eggs	−0.13
Bread	Milk and Cream	−0.28

5 Below is a table of the National Food Survey Committee's estimates of certain income elasticities for the period 1975–1980.

Income elasticities of expenditure

Product	**1975**	**1980**
Liquid milk	0.02	0.06
Natural cheese	0.26	0.48
Beef and veal	0.25	0.47
Mutton and lamb	0.21	0.19
Pork	0.39	0.44
Beef sausages	−0.10	−0.27
Canned meat products	−0.17	−0.27

a Comment on and suggest explanations for these figures.

b Suggest explanations for the following estimates of the income elasticities of household food expenditure:

Type of household	**1975**	**1978**	**1980**
2 adults only (housewife under 55)	−0.04	−0.09	−0.03
2 adults and 3 children	0.20	0.24	0.19

c In the light of the figures contained in this question what do you consider to be the main influences on income elasticity?

7

Markets, revenue and prices

Demand and Revenue

One reason for our interest in demand is its importance for the sales revenue of business firms. Any movement in demand or in quantity demanded will have an effect on the sales revenue of the suppliers. It is a common error of students to imagine that any increase in quantity sold must also increase the seller's sales revenue. This, as we shall see is not the case. We need to examine the effects of changes much more carefully.

Total Revenue

The total revenue achieved at any given price and quantity level will be found by multiplying quantity sold by the price (TR = P × Q). In Fig. 7.1b total revenue at various price levels derived from the demand curve of Fig. 7.1a is shown.

Price £		*Quantity sold* *units*		*Total revenue* £
16	×	2	=	32
10	×	5	=	50
6	×	7	=	42

As the price level changes so, of course, will the total revenue. This is because the quantity sold is changing so that at each different price and quantity level there is a completely new total. This is illustrated in Fig. 7.1 where the total revenue reaches a maximum at price £10 per unit and an output level of 5 units. No other price-quantity combination gives such a good revenue result. You will see that this maximum total revenue occurs at the price of £10. This is the level where, on the same curve featured in Fig. 6.3 the price elasticity of demand was at unity. This is not accidental as we shall now see.

Marginal and Average Revenue

After marginal utility and marginal cost you should already have realised that the term marginal revenue refers to the change in total revenue

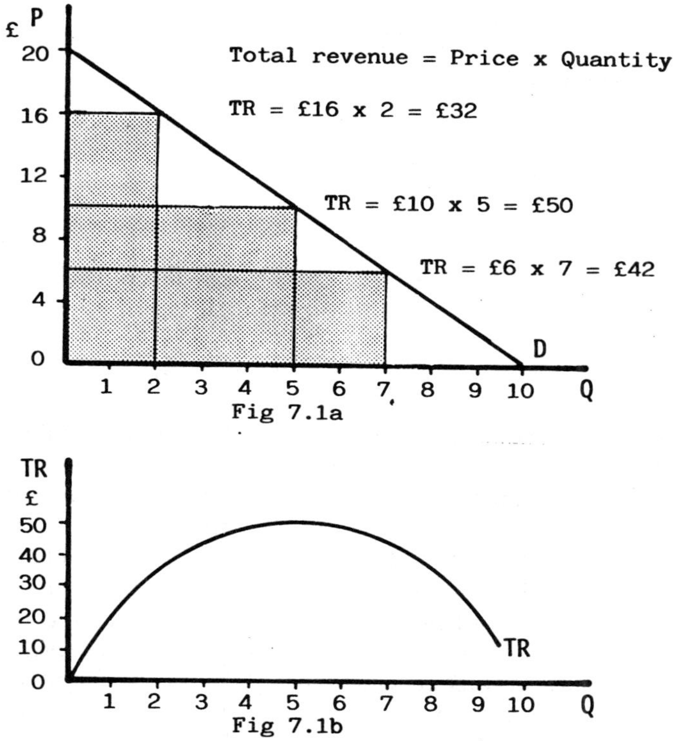

Fig. 7.1 Demand and revenue
The price-quantity relationship of Fig. 7.1a produces the total revenue curve of Fig. 7.1b. This reaches its peak half way between the point of origin (o) and the point where demand = 0. TR is at its maximum when MR = 0 and $E_d = -1$.

generated by a change in sales, usually related to the smallest identifiable unit. For the mathematicians, marginal revenue is the first derivative of total revenue with respect to quantity or output, i.e.:

$$MR = \frac{\partial TR}{\partial Q}$$

where: TR = total revenue and Q = the quantity or output level.

Using the above figures, we can produce a table to illustrate the marginal revenue for each level of weekly output from 1 to 10 units. Notice that the price column is also headed ‘average revenue’, because we assumed that all units were sold at the same price. Total revenue, therefore, equals price multiplied by quantity (TR = P × Q).

1 *Average revenue* £	*2* *Quantity* *units*	*3 (1 × 2)* *Total revenue* £	*Δ3* *Marginal revenue* £
20	0	0	
			18
18	1	18	
			14
16	2	32	
			10
14	3	42	
			6
12	4	48	
			2
10	5	50	
			−2
8	6	48	
			−6
6	7	42	
			−10
4	8	32	
			−14
2	9	18	
			−18
0	10	0	

The marginal revenue column has been positioned at the midpoints of the quantity change in order to emphasise that it relates to a change from one output level to the next. This is how the marginal revenue curve must be plotted on a graph.

Look carefully at the table and at the shape of the graph of Fig. 7.1b. What do you notice about the shape of the total revenue curve? If you do not know why it rises to a peak and then declines, consult your teacher.

Now observe the changes in the average and the marginal revenues with each step in output. Average revenue falls in steps of 2. Marginal revenue falls in steps of 4. This indicates that the marginal revenue curve will slope in the same direction as average revenue and start at the same point on the revenue (vertical) axis but will be exactly twice as steep. This is an important rule which you must remember. It applies whenever the average revenue curve is linear. This is shown graphically in Fig. 7.2. The marginal revenue cuts the quantity axis at 5 units where price is 10, exactly half way to the quantity level (10) where average revenue is 0. The application of a little geometry provides a simple proof.

Total revenue is average revenue multiplied by quantity. This, for the quantity level of 5 units, is represented in Fig. 7.2 by the rectangle MQRO. Total revenue at the quantity level of 5 units is also the sum of all the marginal revenues from 0 to 5 units (18 + 14 + 10 + 6 + 2 = 50). The areas of the rectangle and of the triangle LRO are, therefore, equal. Because the shaded area MNRO is common to both, the areas of the two right angled triangles, LNM and NQR, must also be equal. Elementary geometry proves that the angles of these triangles are equal. Therefore, MN = NQ. Consequently the marginal revenue curve must bisect the dotted line from price 10 to the average revenue. This will be true for any quantity level so the marginal revenue must always bisect the horizontal distance from the price axis to the average revenue curve.

The quantity level where marginal revenue is 0 has a further significance.

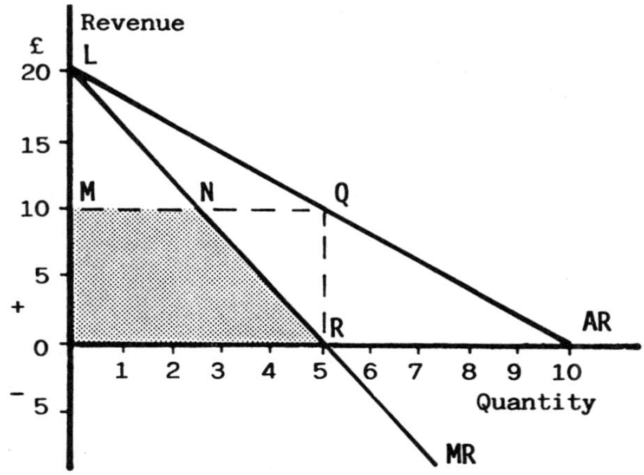

Fig 7.2 The relationship between average and marginal revenue

MN = NQ and the linear marginal revenue curve bisects the distance between the linear average revenue curve and the revenue axis. The linear marginal revenue curve slopes exactly twice as steeply as the average revenue curve.

Look again at Fig. 6.3. Price elasticity of demand for a price change around a midpoint of £10 was shown to have a value of unity. This is not surprising. If the marginal revenue at this quantity point is 0 then a price change around it does not change total revenue. Thus when marginal revenue equals 0, a proportional change in price produces the same proportional change in quantity and price elasticity of demand is −1. Consequently, total revenue remains unchanged and at its peak.

We see then why so much importance is attached to the price level at which the marginal revenue is 0. **This is the level where total revenue is at its maximum and where price elasticity of demand is −1**. At higher price levels, demand is price elastic and a reduction in price will increase total revenue. At lower price levels, demand is price inelastic and a reduction in price will reduce total revenue.

So far we have considered only cases where the firm can increase sales by reducing price. If the firm provides only a very small proportion of the total supply going to the market then the price is unlikely to be affected by any change in the quantity that it sells. This firm is able to sell all it can produce at the market price. Each successive unit increase in quantity is sold at the market price which is, therefore, the same as both the average and the marginal revenue. Graphically this is represented by a linear curve parallel to the quantity axis, as in Fig. 7.3a. This indicates that quantity sold is not dependent upon, or a function of, price. This does not, of course, mean that the price never changes. It can and does change in response to the

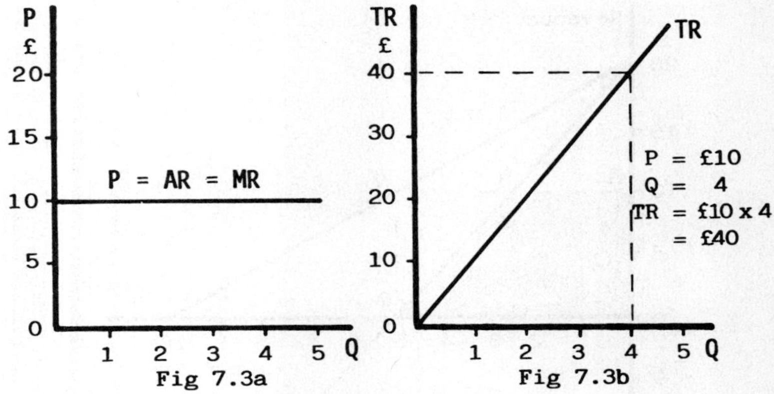

Fig. 7.3 The total revenue of a price taker
Price remains the same at all output levels so that price equals average revenue which equals marginal revenue. Total revenue continues to increase and does not reach a peak.

wider influences affecting the supply and demand conditions in the market as a whole.

Given that the firm's demand, price, and average and marginal revenue curves conform to the general pattern of Fig. 7.3a then the total revenue curve will continue to increase as the firm's sales increase. It will continue to do so as long as the firm's output has no direct effect on the market price. This produces the linear total revenue curve of Fig. 7.3b.

The conditions depicted in Fig. 7.3a and 7.3b apply whenever the firm is able to sell all it can produce at the prevailing market price. It will also apply whenever the firm is a 'price taker' from some outside source e.g. when the price is established by a large dominant firm or if it is controlled by a price regulating body carrying the authority of a national government or transnational body such as the European Community (EC or commonly, EEC)

Industry Demand

So far we have considered demand relationships as they affect the firm and the products of the firm. We need to distinguish demand for a firm's product from that for the general class of product available to buyers.

We can identify several different dimensions of market. For example, we can talk about the demand for personal transport, for private cars, for British manufactured cars, for the BL Maestro car. Each is subject to similar broad influences but each is likely to be affected differently by these influences. Each will be subject to differing price, cross and income elasticities of demand. It is possible for the demand for cars in general to rise while that for the BL car is falling.

The firm needs to be aware of the demand conditions for the industry in which it operates and for its own products. Indeed the concept of market share is well recognised by business managers who are often as concerned with this as they are with the absolute volume of sales and level of total revenue. In some cases the firm may have little power to shift the demand for the industry's products as a whole but it may be able to improve its share of that total demand by its total marketing strategy, i.e. by its product prices, advertising and relationships with distributors.

The Market and the Market Price

The Economic Market

By market we mean an area within which those wanting to buy a particular good can effectively communicate with those able to offer that good for sale. The force of demand is then able to interact with the force of supply. By market price we mean the price which results from the interaction of all the influences operating on buyers and sellers in the market.

There is no definite limit to the size of an economic market. It can be as small as one room or as large as the world. The important requirement for a market to exist at all is for communication to take place between potential and actual buyers and sellers.

An ideal or perfect economic market exists when there is perfect communication between the forces of supply and demand and when nothing impedes the free interaction between these forces. They alone determine the terms and conditions under which the good is exchanged between suppliers and those wanting and prepared to sacrifice their own resources to obtain the good.

The terms perfect or ideal refer only to the conditions under which supply and demand interact. They do not imply any social or moral approval of the consequences. Indeed we may not find the results socially acceptable and we may wish to modify them. If, however, we do wish to intervene in an economic market it is desirable for us to understand this interaction.

A perfect economic market is closely associated with a particular form of market structure called perfect competition. This will be analysed in Chapter 8 and we shall then identify some further features necessary for a market to qualify for this description.

The Market Equilibrium

An economic market is said to be in equilibrium at the prevailing market price when the demand for a good is just equal to the supply of that good. There is then no force tending towards a price change. If you look again at the influences on both supply and demand you will see that the one variable common to both is the good's own price. It is this variable which serves to bring demand and supply into equilibrium in the market. The concept of equilibrium does assume that all the non-price influences on supply and demand are being held constant. Any change in these leading to a shift in either or both of the price-quantity schedules will, of course, change the equilibrium price and quantity.

A simple illustration is provided by combining the supply and demand schedules used for Figs. 4.2 and 6.1 in Chapters 4 and 6:

Price per unit £	*Quantity (units per time period)* *demanded by buyers*	*supplied by sellers*
2	1000	
3	900	100
4	800	200
5	700	300
6	600	400
7	**500**	**500**
8	400	600
9		700

This table is represented by the graph of Fig. 7.4. Both the table and the graph show clearly that there is only one quantity level where the wants of buyers just coincide with the intentions of suppliers. This is at the price of £7 per unit where the quantity supplied equals the quantity demanded at 500 units. This is the **equilibrium price and quantity level**.

This equilibrium is reached by a process of trial and error. If the price happens to be £8, we can see from the diagram that there is excess supply of 200 units. To avoid accumulating unsaleable stocks, firms reduce price and, in effect, 'slide down their supply curves'. As the price falls consumers slide down their demand curves. If we start from a lower price, say £6, the opposite process takes place. At this price demand is greater than supply. Consumers will be prepared to pay more and suppliers to charge more and once again the price moves towards the equilibrium level.

Suppose some authority, **without taking any other measures to influence the wants of buyers and the intentions of suppliers**, tries to impose a price other than £7. If it sets a price of £6, buyers will be trying to buy 600 units per week in a market supplied only with 400 units. There is a shortfall of 200 units or excess demand of 200. The authority will have to decide how to allocate available supply and on what basis to determine which buyers are to be disappointed.

If, on the other hand, the authority tried to set a price of £8 per unit suppliers would be trying to sell 600 units to a market willing to buy only 400. At this price there is excess supply of 200 units. The authority again has an allocation problem of deciding what to do with the 200 units that nobody wants to buy at the prevailing price.

Either condition leads to problems and distortions. If demand is greater than supply some people (those for whom the money equivalent marginal utility is higher than the current price) will be prepared to offer a higher price even when this is against the law. An illicit or 'black' market is likely to develop and the authority will find itself increasingly involved in measures to enforce the law.

If supply is greater than demand then the surplus has to be disposed of somehow. The European Community has been known to destroy apples, and surplus wine is regularly converted to vinegar. Surpluses cannot be stored indefinitely and some may have to be sold eventually at a price well below the market equilibrium. What the authority will not wish to do, if for political reasons it wants prices to be high, will be to allow the surplus product to return to the market where it would help to maintain the imbalance of demand and supply. However immoral it may appear, the authority is likely to try to remove the surplus completely from the market area, if necessary by destruction.

The Community farm support system is based on the establishment of regulated prices which, for the most part, apply to both suppliers and buyers. We may compare this with an alternative system which was, in fact, in force in Great Britain before her entry to the EEC. This was based on an agreed guaranteed minimum price for producers. The Government paid a subsidy to the producers of a farm product if the market price of that product fell below the level of the guaranteed minimum.

The Community system sets a regulated price above the market equilibrium so that, as explained above, demand is lower and supply higher than would be the case without regulation. It encourages over-production and consumption is discouraged by high prices.

The former British system allowed a market equilibrium price to be established and this, for the most part, was the price paid by the consumer. Any shortfall between market price and the guaranteed minimum was paid to the producer in the form of a subsidy. This sytem created fewer market distortions than those produced by a regulated market price.

Changes in Market Equilibrium

Changes in Demand and Supply

In previous chapters we have seen that there can be shifts in the demand or supply price-quantity schedules and, consequently, shifts in the demand and supply curves. These can arise through changes in any of the variables which affect both supply and demand or because of changes in the prices of other goods.

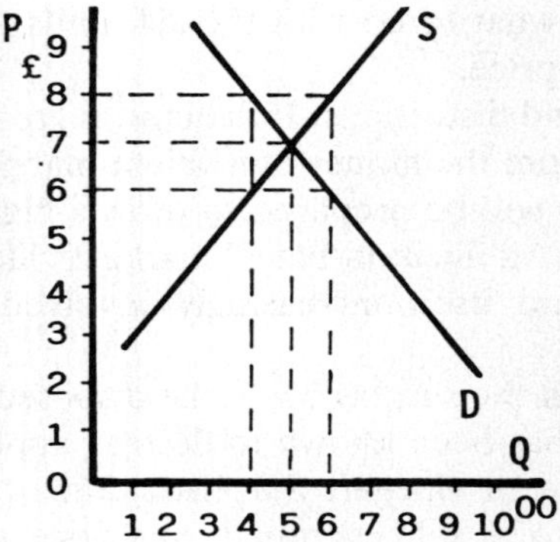

Fig. 7.4 The equilibrium price and quantity
Only at price £7 do the intentions of suppliers match those of buyers.

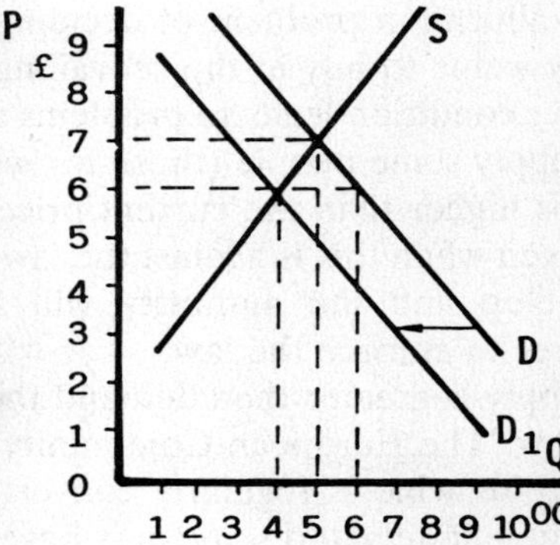

Fig. 7.5 A shift in the demand curve and change in equilibrium price
The curve shifts from **D** to $\mathbf{D_1}$ and the equilibrium price falls from £7 to £6.

Figs. 7.5 and 7.6 illustrate the effect of such shifts. Notice that Fig. 7.5 represents a change which reduces demand. This, for example, might be brought about by a fall in income, a rise in the price of a complementary good or simply a change in taste against the product. The result, however, is that buyers want to buy less of the good at each price. As the supply schedule remains unchanged, the equilibrium price at which the quantity supplied equalled quantity demanded falls from £7 to £6.

Fig. 7.6 represents a change in the influences on supply so that suppliers are willing to supply a larger quantity at each price. Such a change might be the result of a fall in factor prices, a fall in an indirect tax or some change in the conditions of production that make it less profitable to produce an alternative product. Payment of a subsidy, as shown in Fig. 7.7, has a similar effect. The changes in equilibrium illustrated in these graphs assume that demand influences remain unchanged.

It may have occurred to you that the movement in equilibrium price and quantity depends not only on the extent of the shift in supply or demand but also on the slopes of the curves. Experiment yourself with a ruler and observe the effect of changing the slope of the demand curve in Fig. 7.6 and of the supply curve in Fig. 7.5.

What can you say about the effects on these shifts of changing the slopes? What combination of supply and demand conditions are likely to result in the largest and the smallest changes in equilibrium price?

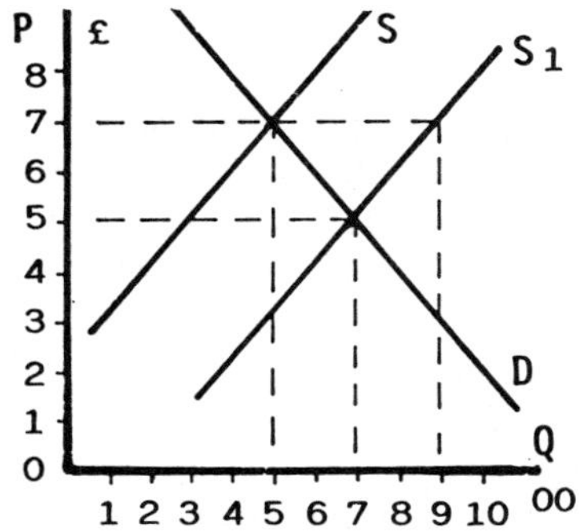

Fig. 7.6 A shift in the supply curve and change in equilibrium price
The supply curve shifts from **S** to **S_1** and the equilibrium price falls from £7 to £5. The equilibrium quantity rises from 500 to 700.

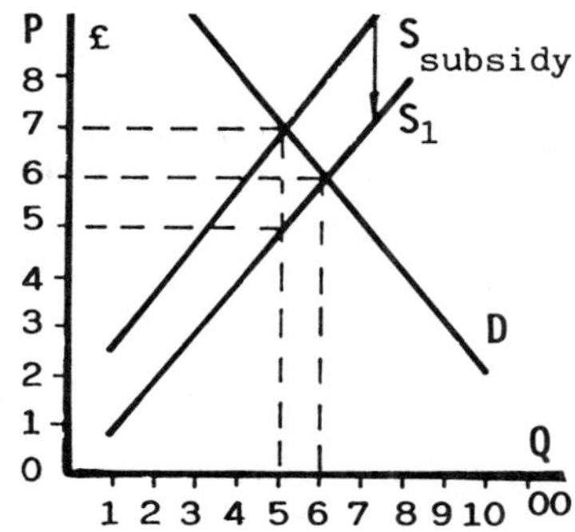

Fig. 7.7 The effect of a subsidy on market equilibrium
A subsidy to producers shifts the supply curve from **S** to **S_1** to bring a reduction in equilibrium price and an increase in market supply.

Reasons for Market Intervention

In Chapter 1 we recognised that a production system based purely on market prices was likely to have serious defects and that some production was likely to become the direct responsibility of the State on behalf of the community as a whole. In addition to some deficiencies in **what is produced**, a completely unregulated market may result in a pattern of **distribution** of goods and services – the **for whom** aspect of production – that does not accord with prevailing views of social justice and worth.

One problem is that all consumers are unlikely to have an equal vote in the democracy of the market-place. People with the biggest incomes will have the most influence on the force of demand and will then have the most influence on the way scarce economic resources are used. The influence of the most powerful buyers in the market may be directed to purely selfish ends with harmful consequences for the community as a whole. No society has yet succeeded in removing all inequalities of consumption and not everyone would agree that total equality was even desirable. Nevertheless, it is difficult to justify large inequalities in the consumption of what society regards as basic goods and services such as housing, food, health care and education. It is not surprising, therefore, that many governments should seek to ensure that such economic goods are available to as many people as possible.

Forms of Market Intervention

What then are the options open to a government which considers that the free or unregulated market is not providing a socially acceptable quantity of a particular good for sections of the community? We have seen that price regulation alone is most unlikely to solve the problem. The Government, either directly or through agencies under its control, could enter the market as a producer and so increase supply. The British Government, for example, has provided health and education services and, through local government authorities, has provided housing. It could seek to redistribute income through taxation and welfare payments and so re-allocate available 'consumer votes'. Most Western European Governments make payments out of taxation to the unemployed, the chronically sick and the old.

Subsidies

These measures, however, may be insufficient or unsuitable for some goods or services. A further possibility is to influence supply by making payments to suppliers in addition to the prices paid by buyers. This is known as paying a **subsidy** to suppliers or producers. Suppose a subsidy of £2 per unit is paid to suppliers of the good represented in Fig. 7.4. The subsidy is an addition to market price so that when the market price is £6, suppliers receive £8, when it is £8, they receive £10, and so on. The supply curve now moves to the right. At a subsidised price of £5, suppliers are now willing to supply the quantity (500 units) for which previously they wanted £7. At a subsidised £7 they supply the quantity (700 units) previously requiring £9. This is shown in Fig. 7.7.

Some people who would or could not buy at the old equilibrium price of £7 may now become buyers as the equilibrium price falls. Assuming that the demand intentions remain unchanged – the demand curve staying the same as that shown in Fig. 7.4 – a new equilibrium is reached at the reduced price of £6. At this new equilibrium price the quantity that firms wish to supply just equals the quantity that consumers wish to buy at a level of 600 units. The amount actually supplied to the market at the equilibrium price thus rises from 500 to 600 units.

Notice that the equilibrium market price has not fallen by the full extent of the subsidy. This would only happen if the demand curve were vertical or if the supply curve were horizontal. Because the demand curve will normally have a negative, and the supply curve a positive, slope the amount of a subsidy change is always likely to have both a price and a quantity effect. The steeper the slopes the greater will be the effect on price. You should experiment with a ruler to find out for yourself the probable results of subsidy changes on products with different supply and demand slopes.

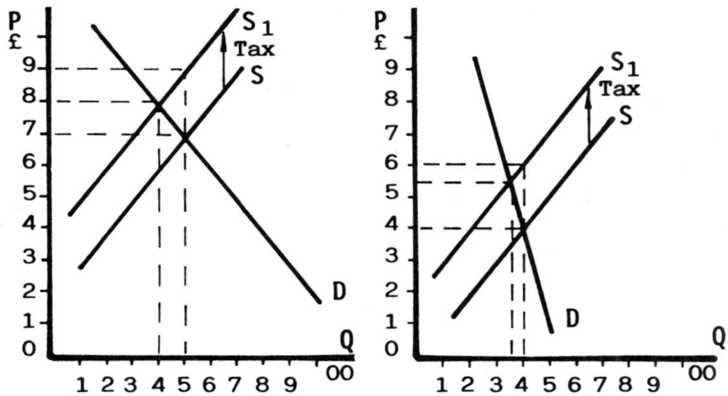

Fig 7.8a Fig 7.8b

Fig. 7.8 The effect of an expenditure tax on market equilibrium
In each case producers pay a tax of £2 per unit and the supply curve shifts from **S** to $\mathbf{S_1}$ indicating that producers are prepared to sell less at each price. In Fig. 7.8a market price rises by £1 and supply to the market falls by 100. In Fig. 7.8b the slope of the demand curve is such that market price rises by £1.50 and market supply falls only by 50. A government seeking to raise revenue taxes markets closer to Fig. 7.8b than to Fig. 7.8a.

Expenditure taxes

Suppose the Government wished to reduce the quantity of a good entering the market. It might, perhaps, consider that the good was harmful to health or undesirable for social reasons. Instead of paying a subsidy, it could impose a tax at some point of production or distribution. The effect of a tax would be the reverse to that of a subsidy and it is illustrated in Figure 7.8, where again an amount of £2 per unit is assumed.

Payment of the tax is required from producers or suppliers to the market and these now require the price plus the amount of tax in order to be willing to supply the former quantity. The supply curve now shifts to the left and the market equilibrium price in Fig. 7.8a rises to £8 at the quantity level where quantity demanded just equals quantity supplied at 400 units per time period. Again the market equilibrium price does not rise by the full amount of the tax because some people are not willing to pay the higher price and stop buying the product. Notice that in this market, any attempt to keep the price unchanged at £7 after the tax imposition would reduce the quantity supplied to 300 units. If, on the other hand suppliers tried to charge a price to include the full amount of tax – £9 – then the quantity demanded would fall to 300 units and there would be an excess supply of 200 as firms continued to supply the old quantity of 500 units.

We should also consider the implications of imposing this tax. We have seen that, given the conditions represented by the supply and demand schedules there is a reduction in quantity supplied to the market. This could be serious for firms if previously they had been operating with small profit margins or if their production processes involved a high proportion of fixed costs. The reduction in output could change profits into losses and some firms could be forced to close with loss of employment opportunities for workers.

Expenditure Taxes, Government Revenue and Production

Suppose, however, the Government did not wish to interfere unduly with production but still wanted to impose a tax because, say, it needed the additional revenue to pay its own employees. It would seek a product that was not very responsive to price changes, i.e. one that was highly price inelastic. The reduction in demand would then be kept to a minimum. A possible situation is illustrated in Fig. 7.8b. Here, the slope of the curve is much less responsive to price changes. The supply curve before tax is S, the equilibrium price £4, and the quantity 400 units per week. After the imposition of a £2 per unit tax the supply curve moves to S_1. The graph illustrates that the equilibrium price rises by most of the amount of the tax (in fact to £5.50) and there is only a small fall in quantity (to 350 units per week). The Government achieves an increase in revenue of £350 × £2 = £700 per week. If this seems too small to be realistic, think of this as representing millions of pounds.

However, would the Government be correct in assuming that it had achieved an increase in its own revenues with very little disruption to production? Certainly there is a little loss of production for this product but we need to look a little further into the consequences of the tax.

The £700 (or £700 m) has to be paid from consumer incomes which would otherwise have been available for spending on other goods and services. If all other conditions remain unchanged, the loss of spendable or disposable income is going to reduce demand in other product markets and the reduction is going to be greatest for those goods with a high income elasticity of demand. If, on the other hand, people resist this reduction in their general spending power and, in the absence of high unemployment, they are able to press for and obtain income compensating wage rises, then producers' wage costs are likely to rise and this will influence their supply intentions.

We can see then that there can be several consequences of any change in taxation and the eventual changes in Government revenue and production may be difficult to predict with any great precision.

Exercises Relating to Chapter 7

1 Choose one model of car in current large-scale production and discuss how demand for this model is likely to differ from the demand for private cars in general.

2 State the objectives of one agricultural support system (e.g. the system adopted in the EEC or in the USA). Describe its method of operation and discuss its consequences for consumer prices and taxes.

3 Discuss the case for treating blood as a normal economic good and letting suply and demand determine its market price.

4 Compare, using economic analysis, the probable consequences of replacing a food production subsidy by an income supplement for low income groups.

5 'In a free market, supply will always equal demand.' Discuss this statement and examine the implication that the regulation of market prices can never be justified.

8

Perfect competition and monopoly

Profit Maximisation

In Chapter 4 we recognised that the modern business company might have objectives other than the maximisation of profit. We should not, however, abandon this objective. On the contrary, it remains the essential starting point for economic analysis. We shall commence our examination of the firm's behaviour in the market place by assuming that the firm is seeking to make the largest possible profit during a single time period. Before we can do so we need to make sure that we understand the conditions that have to be fulfilled for profits to be maximised.

The Importance of Profit Maximisation

In Chapter 2 we defined profit in the simplest possible terms as the balance of the firm's revenue after all costs have been met. To maximise profit, therefore, the firm must achieve the largest possible difference between revenue and costs. The firm can continue to increase its profits by expanding output as long as the additional revenue it earns from each successive unit increase in output is greater than the cost of producing that unit. This is simply to say that it will pay the firm to increase output as long as marginal revenue is greater than marginal cost. If marginal cost is greater than marginal revenue then the firm will make a greater profit by reducing output. It should do so, therefore, until marginal revenue is equal to marginal cost.

This is illustrated very simply in Fig. 8.1 where the firm is able to sell all the output it can produce at the prevailing market (or regulated) price. An unregulated market price is the result of the interaction of market forces as described in Chapter 7. A regulated price may be set by a Government or by a market authority which has the legal powers to do so. An example would be prices established under the Common Agricultural Policy (CAP), of the EEC.

Assuming that the firm can sell all its product at the same price and that the price is not influenced by any changes in its output, then average revenue equals marginal revenue. If the firm is producing at quantity level

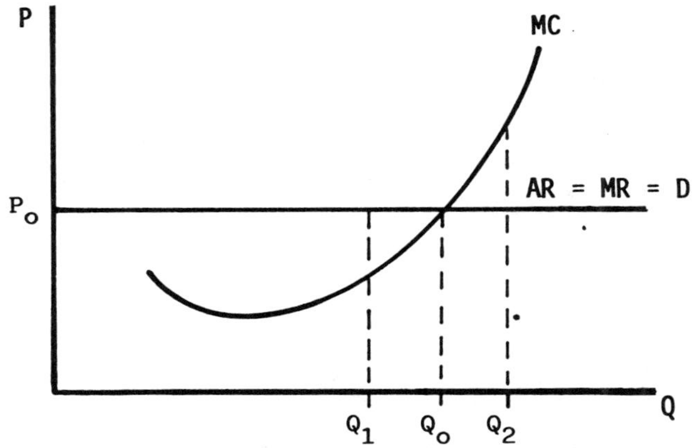

Fig. 8.1 Profit maximisation for the price taker
Only at Q_0 where **MR** = **MC** will it not pay the firm to change its production level. Profits, therefore, are maximised at Q_0.

Q_1 then marginal revenue is still more than the rising marginal cost and it will pay to increase output. If it is producing at quantity level Q_2 marginal cost is higher than marginal revenue and profit will be increased by reducing output. Profit will be at its maximum possible level or, if price is lower than average total cost, the loss will be at its lowest possible level, when marginal revenue equals marginal cost at quantity Q_0.

Exactly the same argument holds good for the firm in the situation illustrated by Fig. 8.2. Here, the demand varies with the price charged by the firm. If the firm reduces the product's price it will be able to sell an increased quantity. The average and marginal revenue curves are both downward sloping as explained in Chapter 6. Remember we also explained that the slope of the marginal revenue curve was twice as steep as that of the average revenue curve. The profit maximising, or loss minimising quantity is still Q_0, where marginal revenue equals marginal cost but the price at this quantity is P_0 as indicated in the diagram.

At this stage you should also check that you understand the difference between **profit** and **revenue**. Profit, of course, is the balance of revenue after all costs have been paid. In Fig. 8.2, the revenue maximising quantity level is Q_3 at price P_3. If you do not know why, you should revise Chapter 7 very carefully. What can you say about the price elasticities of demand at prices P_0 and P_3? If you are not sure of the answer, refer to Chapters 6 and 7 or consult your teacher. These points are thoroughly rehearsed in the computer exercises of section 7 of the disc.

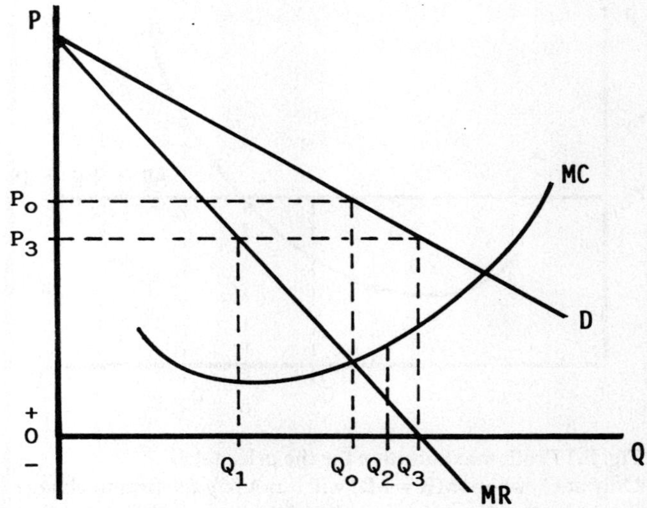

Fig. 8.2 Profit maximisation for the price maker
Profit maximisation is achieved at Q_0 where **MR** = **MC**.
Revenue maximisation is achieved at Q_3 where **MR** = 0.

Perfect Competition

Conditions for Perfect Competition

It is a fundamental assumption in economics that the behaviour of a business organisation will be influenced by the structure of the market in which it is operating. By structure we generally mean anything that influences buyers or sellers for example, the extent of competition provided by other suppliers or possible suppliers of the good under consideration and the relationship existing between the suppliers and buyers in the market. Clearly there are very many possible market structures. At introductory levels of economics, however, we are normally concerned with a limited number of widely recognised though rather stylised structures.

One extreme form of market structure is called **perfect competition**. For this to exist certain strict conditions have to be fulfilled. These are as follows:

1 The number of suppliers and potential suppliers must be large in relation to demand but the size of individual suppliers must be small. This ensures that the likely output level provided by any individual supplier is not sufficient on its own to influence significantly total market supply and, thereby, the equilibrium price. It is also necessary to stipulate that

it must not be possible for groups of suppliers to band together in order to influence the market price.

2 Similar conditions to those stipulated for supply in **1** must apply to buyers and potential buyers in the market.

3 The good must be perceived as being the same good with the same qualities, whatever the source of supply. Buyers must be indifferent as to the source of supply. Goods with this quality are said to be **homogeneous**.

4 Communications within the market must be perfect. No section of supply or demand must have access to information not also immediately available to all other sections of the market. Transport is also assumed to be costless and the good is assumed to be accessible on equal terms at all points within the market. It is an important consequence of this assumption that no one supplier has any technical or marketing superiority over any other supplier.

5 The motivation of buyers and sellers is assumed to be purely economic. This 'economic motivation' is considered to be 'self interest', expressed as the desire to **maximise profits** on the part of supplying organisations and to **maximise utility** on the part of consumers or consumer households. There is no intrusion of 'non-economic' motives such as a desire to serve the public, patriotism, sympathy for the sick or ambition for social prestige or political power.

6 There are no barriers preventing entry to or exit from the market. Both suppliers and buyers must be free to enter and leave the market as they wish in accordance with their own self-interest. This freedom of entry and exit must also apply to the production factors employed by suppliers. Firms are not free to enter and leave a market unless they are also able to hire and dismiss the factors of production, including workers.

These, of course, are extreme conditions which are unlikely to be found in practice. For this reason economists are sometimes criticised for continuing to retain the concept of perfect competition. However, by setting up an idealised model it is possible to study the 'pure' effect of economic forces. Only when these are properly understood is it possible to identify the true consequences of the various **imperfections** found in the real world. We can compare this with the physicist's desire to have a laboratory in space where experiments can be conducted entirely free from polluting effect of the earth's atmosphere. These experiments can teach the physicist much about the effect of the earth's influence on the behaviour of materials. The economist's studies of perfect competition help him to understand the effects of 'pollution' in actual markets.

Firms under Perfect Competition

In the perfectly competitive market, the firm has to accept the market price over which it has no influence. It also has to accept the market level of technology and of factor costs (wages, interest rates, rent and input prices). As its assumed objective is to maximise profits, its main decision problem lies in choosing its optimum output level which will be where marginal cost is equal to marginal revenue which, here, is also equal to price. We also assume that we are considering short-run adjustments so that we are concerned with short-run cost conditions. The short run, you should remember, is that period during which it is not possible to increase all the factors of production so that at least one remains fixed.

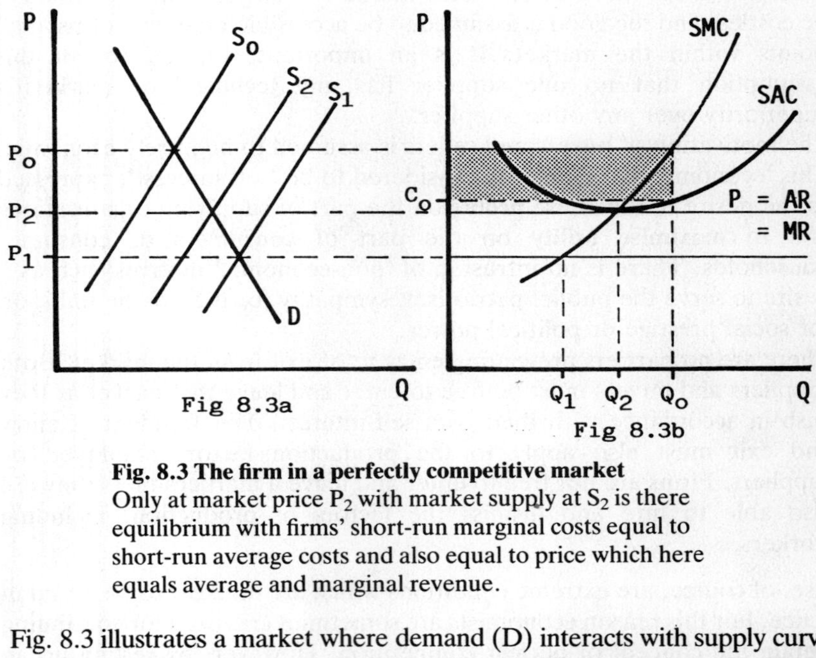

Fig. 8.3 The firm in a perfectly competitive market
Only at market price P_2 with market supply at S_2 is there equilibrium with firms' short-run marginal costs equal to short-run average costs and also equal to price which here equals average and marginal revenue.

Fig. 8.3 illustrates a market where demand (D) interacts with supply curves S_0, S_2 and S_1 to produce a range of market equilibrium prices, P_0, P_2 and P_1. The market equilibrium was explained in Chapter 7. It is defined as the condition existing when the market price is at the level where the quantity supplied to the market just equals the quantity demanded. The equilibrium price is also known as the 'market clearing price', i.e. the price at which total supply is just taken up by buyers in the market.

This is carried through into Fig. 8.3b which shows the position of the individual firm. Here the initial market price is high enough to enable the firm to secure a profit over and above the return to all factors of production. At this stage we shall refer to this as a **super-normal profit** but see the appendix, A Note on Profit, at the end of this chapter. You will notice in Fig. 8.3 that at price P_0 the firm will produce output Q_0 and enjoy a super-normal profit of P_0–C_0 for each unit of the good sold. The total profit, in this sense, is represented by the shaded area. In the traditional analysis of perfect competition, 'enterprise' is included as a production factor and an element of 'normal profit' as a payment to enterprise is included as a cost. Thus, any excess of average revenue (price) over average cost is regarded as super-normal profit – a surplus belonging to, but not strictly earned by, the entrepreneur, the supplier of enterprise.

If one firm can earn super-normal profit, then, given the assumption of perfect communications, so can all the others. The existence of such a profitable market will attract other suppliers. The consequent increase in total supply will shift the market supply curve to the right and, assuming that demand is unchanged, the equilibrium price will fall.

If the market price falls below P_2, e.g. to P_1, it will be below the minimum average cost and the individual firm (and all others in the market) will suffer a short-run loss. Firms will not stay in a market where there are losses and those with more profitable opportunities elsewhere will move out. Some may go out of business altogether. The result will be a fall in total market supply. This process of supply adjustment may continue until individual firms are making neither losses nor pure profits. Supply is in equilibrium when the average cost curve is at a tangent to market price as experienced by the individual firm. This is at market price P_2 at which price the firm produces output Q_2. Because pure profit and losses have been eliminated, there are no longer any incentives for firms to enter or leave this particular market. The firm can then be said to be in an equilibrium position because there is no longer any pressure to adjust its output level.

Super-normal profit is eliminted and at the equilibrium level of output for the individual firm, Q_2, the market price equals the firm's average revenue. It is also equal to its marginal revenue, its average cost and its marginal cost.

The firm, we do have to remember, is seeking to maximise profit and to do this, must produce at the output level where its marginal cost is equal to marginal revenue which, here, is the market price.

If you cannot see why these equalities exist you should revise very carefully the chapter sections 3.1 and 7.1 concerned with short-run costs and revenue. Remember, the average cost is at its minimum and the firm can sell all it can produce at the market price.

There is a further equality in this equilibrium position. The price resulting from the interaction of market forces represents the money equivalent of the utility of the last or marginal consumer – the one who buys the last unit of market supply. We can say, then, that market price equals marginal utility. If this is not clear you should revise Chapter 5.

We now have the condition where the money equivalent of marginal utility also equals marginal cost. The value placed on the last unit supplied to the market just equals the cost of producing that unit. We show in

Chapter 11 that this is often regarded as a desirable condition from the point of view of consumer welfare.

The market is also considered to be making efficient use of production resources because firms are forced to operate at the output where average costs are at their lowest. This is sometimes called the **optimum output position** because of the efficiency of resource use – at least in the short run. Notice that in the equilibrium situation the firm is obliged to adopt profit maximising behaviour and to seek to equate marginal cost and marginal revenue because any other output level will bring about a loss. Only when it produces at Q_2 in Fig. 8.3 can it survive in the market.

The Firm's Supply under Perfect Competition

The above analysis can also indicate how the supply curve of the individual firm operating under these conditions may be derived. Remember the essential condition for profit maximisation, that marginal revenue should be equal to marginal cost. Remember too, that in this perfectly competitive market marginal revenue equals average revenue which equals price. The firm, then, will adjust its output to any change in price in accordance with its marginal cost schedule. Look again at Fig. 8.3. At price P_1 the firm produces output Q_1; at price P_2 quantity produced rises to Q_2 and at P_0 the quantity is Q_0.

If we were to reproduce this price-quantity schedule in the form of a supply curve for the firm we would simply reproduce its marginal cost curve. Normally, we are concerned only with the range of prices and quantities where the rising marginal cost curve is above the average variable cost curve. It is technically possible to have an equilibrium position where the average variable cost curve is falling but this would mean that price was lower than average variable cost and it would be cheaper to close down rather than continue production. If you are not certain about these cost relationships you should revise Chapter 3.

Consequences of Perfect Competition

However desirable the perfectly competitive market may appear to be from the consumer's or the community's point of view, it is an extremely uncomfortable situation for the producer who must constantly adjust output levels and his own demand for factors. Fig. 8.3 represents only a partial equilibrium. It is a condition where there is no pressure to change supply. It says nothing about demand. A change in demand from any of the influences listed in Chapter 6 will immediately upset the market equilibrium. Price will respond to a shift in the market demand curve and firms in the market are able to make super-normal profits or will suffer losses once more. We would have to predict that, following a shift in demand and a change in market price, the supply and price adjustment process illustrated in Fig. 8.3 will start again. Because price equals marginal revenue and because survival in the market requires firms to seek the output level where marginal cost equals marginal revenue, shifting prices force firms to keep adjusting output.

It is not surprising that the closer a market approaches to perfect competition the more volatile is the price. The Stock Exchange and the London Commodity Exchanges are often quoted as examples of markets containing many features of perfect competition. In these markets, prices are constantly fluctuating.

Modern manufacturing, which requires long-term planning and which involves very heavy fixed costs, finds it extremely difficult to tolerate fluctuating prices. If the market price falls below the level of average costs, firms, as we have seen, suffer losses. They can survive in the short run as long as price does not fall below average **variable** cost. Some fixed costs can be postponed for a time and firms may be able to draw on capital reserves to a limited extent. However, in the long run firms cannot survive unless **all** costs are covered, i.e. unless price is at least equal to the minimum of the average total costs, including 'normal' profit.

Producers, especially those in manufacturing, who find themselves operating in markets approximating to perfect competition will seek to change the market structure by all means available to them. The existence of substantial internal economies of scale as explained earlier in the course, tends to result in industries with a limited number of suppliers. Most markets, therefore, represent some form of 'imperfect competition'. Before examining these, however, it is helpful to go to the other market extreme, that of **monopoly**

Monopoly

Conditions of Monopoly

Monopoly is the condition where the market supply of a good is provided entirely by one organisation or group of organisations operating to common rules.

The starting point of discussions on monopoly is usually that of the traditional model in which the monopolist is assumed to be pursuing an objective of profit maximisation. The model is essentially short run and depicts rising marginal costs. It is presented in the graph of Fig. 8.4.

The Firm as a Monopolist

In addition to the points already made the following features of this model should be observed:

1 The firm must be able to preserve its monopoly position from potential

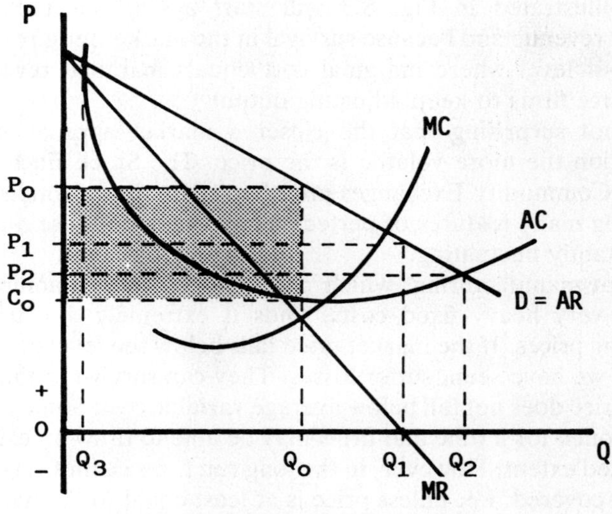

Fig. 8.4 Monopoly assuming profit maximisation
Profit maximisation is achieved at output Q_0 where profits are the shaded area $Q_0 \times (P_0 - C_0)$. Revenue is maximised at Q_1 and profits can be made at any output level between Q_3 and Q_2.

entrants to the market. There must, therefore be some effective barriers to the entry of new firms to the market. These barriers may be natural or artificial.

Natural barriers
These arise from the conditions of production. For example, the ability to supply a particular product or service may depend on possession of a unique ingredient, item of knowledge or skill. Alternatively production may require capital on a scale so large that a community's financial resources can support only one supplier.

Artificial barriers
These may be legal in origin. Governments have always had the power to grant monopolies. Kings of England once regarded this power as an important source of income! More recently, State-owned industries and services have been granted monopolies. The Post Office, for example, has the sole right to supply most forms of letter post. The patent laws grant approved patent holders a monopoly for a limited period in the application of certain inventions. In this case, monopoly is granted in return for the disclosure of knowledge to the State. Other barriers may be erected by the monopolist, perhaps in collusion with other producers who agree to share markets so that each becomes a sole supplier to a part

of the market. The enjoyment of those internal economies of scale, identified in earlier chapters, especially the substantial economies of advertising, may enable a producer to extend and preserve monopoly power. Some of these producer-created barriers can be remarkably long-lived in spite of official attempts to remove them or make them illegal.

2 The firm's production is the total supply to the market. The market demand is thus also the demand curve for the monopolist and can be assumed to be downward sloping as shown. Assuming that all units at any given quantity level are sold at the same price, then the demand curve is also the average revenue curve. At this stage, we should also note that the existence of monopoly always relates to a defined market area. Any change in the size of the market area, resulting perhaps from a change in communications, may threaten the monopoly. A village store will lose its monopoly of local retailing if an efficient transport service is provided to a nearby town. A national supplier of any consumer product loses monopoly power if imports become readily available and fashionable. Large firms operating in many markets may be monopolists in some but face fierce competition in others.

3 The marginal revenue curve lies below the average revenue curve and, when linear, slopes twice as steeply.

4 The profit maximising output level, where marginal revenue equals marginal cost is at output Q_0 and the market clearing price is P_0.

5 Although it is possible for a monopolist to suffer losses, especially in the public sector where objectives other than profit may be important, the model normally assumes that the private sector monopolist will not trouble to maintain a monopoly unless this is profitable. We, therefore, normally show the average cost curve below the average revenue curve at the profit maximising output level. On this basis it is argued that the monopolist will make super-normal profits represented by the shaded area formed by $Q_0 \times (P_0 - C_0)$. Average, or unit, cost at level C_0 includes normal profit as previously defined, so that any excess of unit price (P_0) over cost (C_0) equals super-normal profit ($P_0 - C_0$). The total of this will be the number of units sold (Q_0) $\times$ ($P_0 - C_0$). As in the case of perfect competition it is assumed that costs include returns to all production factors, including a normal profit element as payment for entrepreneurial or organisational skill. The super-normal profit is thus a surplus arising out of the monopoly market structure and maintained as long as the barriers to market entry are preserved.

Supply under Monopoly

Even if we assume profit maximising behaviour we are unable to identify the supply curve for a monopolist. There is no single relationship between price and quantity supplied as there is in perfect competition. The profit maximising output depends on marginal cost and marginal revenue and the position of the marginal revenue curve depends on the demand-average revenue curve. In order to predict output we have to know the demand curve as well as the marginal cost curve. It is possible to have different demand curves where the same price is associated with different profit maximising output levels or where the same output level is associated with different prices. You should test this statement for yourself by drawing several linear demand curves with varying slopes and working out the profit maximising prices and output levels. Remember that the marginal revenue curve cuts the quantity axis half way between the point of origin and the quantity level where $AR = 0$.

Consequences of Monopoly

On the basis of the above features monopolists are frequently accused of:

a Making profits which they have not earned.
b Charging prices which are above marginal costs and thus causing a 'deadweight welfare loss' as explained in Chapter 11.

These are the main criticisms on which much anti-monopoly (also known as anti-trust) policy is based. There are defences against these criticisms and the case against the monopoly model is by no means conclusive. In particular the average total cost curve is drawn in quite an arbitrary manner. Its position is not derived from the marginal cost curve but is dependent on the level of fixed costs and the ratio of fixed to variable costs. Because the monopolist may be enjoying economies of scale as a result of employing modern capital equipment giving rise to fixed costs, this may have an important bearing on any cost comparisons with competitive markets which lack scale economies.

We return to this problem in Chapter 11 when we examine public policy towards monopolies and large firms with significant market power.

Some doubt is cast on the assumption that monopolists will always seek to maximise profits. While profit maximising behaviour, whether firms realise this or not, can be said to be a survival condition of perfect competition this is not true for a monopoly. The monopolist can survive at any output level between the two break-even points where average cost equals average revenue, points Q_3 and Q_2 in Fig. 8.4. This means that the monopolist can still make profits if he decides to increase output above the profit maiximising level of Q_0 up to Q_2. This gives him the freedom to pursue other objectives – revenue, rather than profit maximisation, for example. In the model of Fig. 8.4 revenue is maximised at output Q_1 and at price P_1 where marginal revenue equals 0. Such an objective would not eliminate the criticisms based on the conventional monopoly model but it would reduce their force. A revenue maximising output must always be higher and the price lower than that required for profit maximisation unless marginal costs are 0, an unlikely situation.

The stability of a monopoly depends on how it is preserved and the strength of entry barriers. If the monopoly was created by law as in the case of the Post Office or the National Coal Board then it can only be changed by legal and political processes. A number of public sector monopolies including some operated by British Telecom were opened up to private sector competition in the early 1980s. Patent laws, which give monopoly rights over certain processes for a limited period, can always be changed by government process; in Britain this means by an Act of Parliament.

A private sector monopoly, depending on barriers to market entry, is stable as long as the barriers remain effective. In practice, they can never be permanent. If the profit incentive is sufficiently powerful, firms will seek to undermine or get round them in a variety of ways including the development of products which are physically different from those supplied by the monopolist but which offer similar utility, i.e. carry out similar functions. Monopolies are at their most vulnerable in a period of technological change when new products and processes are being developed and when market boundaries are being extended by developments in transport and communications.

Traditionally, monopolies have tended to be considered within a framework of national markets. Today, of course, we have to recognise that a growing number of markets are world wide or extend to transnational groups such as the EC. Very large multinational companies are still likely to seek to gain monopoly power in these expanded market areas. These trends present economists with new questions for the examination of markets and entry barriers and they also pose new problems in the development of business law.

Complete monopoly, involving total control over supply to a market is uncommon in the private sector and the majority of markets lie between the extremes of perfect competition and monopoly. Aspects of these imperfect market structures are examined in Chapter 9.

Exercises Relating to Chapter 8

1 Explain why a firm cannot charge a price at which its product's demand is price inelastic and at the same time be maximising its profits.

2 Why is perfect competition an uncomfortable market for producers? How can a producer try to achieve a more comfortable market structure?

3 Explain as fully as possible, and with the help of diagrams, why it is not possible to predict a supply curve for a monopolist.

4 Discuss the case for maintaining a monopoly for the provision of telephone and telecommunication services.

5 'Advertising is a sign of healthy competition.' 'Advertising is a powerful force protecting established suppliers against possible competition.' Discuss these apparently conflicting statements.

Appendix: A Note on Profit

Profit is one of those common terms which presents considerable difficulties when we begin to examine it closely. At the simplest level we can say that revenue – cost = profit. Then we have to define cost and here our problems start. We have to decide whether or not to include as a cost some return to a possible fourth production factor such as enterprise. If we do then we have to decide precisely what we mean by enterprise and what constitutes a normal return to this as an element in the production process.

J. Harvey appears to approach the problem along these lines in his *Elementary Economics*. Harvey points out that part of what is generally called the 'profit' of an 'entrepreneur' includes income for his labour. Any excess is made up partly of normal profit which he defines as 'what is just sufficient to keep the entrepreneur in the industry' and partly of 'abnormal profit' which is defined as an addition gained 'because, in the short period, other persons cannot enter competition with him'. A major weakness of this view of abnormal profit as a reward for a kind of temporary monopoly is its apparent total disregard for corporate profits.

Textbook writers sometimes use the term super-normal instead of abnormal. F. Livesey, for example in his *Textbook of Economics* notes that marginal analysis usually includes within cost 'an element of profit (normal profit)' which he does not define, but then goes on to say that 'any excess (of profit) is abnormal or super-normal'. The same writer does make a passing definition of normal profit in another book of his, *Economics*, when he examines attempts by firms to seek profits 'greater than the level that would be considered normal or adequate by the majority of firms'. Livesey clearly sees the search for super-normal profit as a normal and common business activity not necessarily related to monopoly.

R. G. Lipsey in his widely used *Introduction to Positive Economics* uses yet another term for profit beyond the normal and offers rather different definitions. He writes of 'pure profit' and defines this as 'any excess of revenues over all opportunity cost'. In his analysis, pure profit is what is left when from revenue is deducted 'the cost of all factors of production other than capital'. Then he further deducts 'the pure return on capital and any risk premium necessary to compensate the owners of capital for the risks associated with its use in this firm and industry'. This is clearly an interpretation more adapted to corporate enterprise and moves beyond the difficult concept of the entrepreneur. It is in keeping with the legal position in which the company is 'owned' by the providers of equity capital. It is still difficult to reconcile with the reality of a stock market where the yield on ordinary shares is often less than that obtainable for fixed interest bearing loan stock holders who have no rights of ownership nor any right to share in profit.

A much more thorough discussion of profit is contained in Samuelson's well-known *Economics*. Samuelson puts forward six separate 'views' and recognises that 'statistical profits' (R–C) are a 'hodgepodge of different elements'. His **first** view consists of 'implied returns' to factors, i.e. factor opportunity costs which are recorded as profits rather than as rent, interest or wages simply because of the vagaries of accounting conventions.

The **second** view is the 'reward to enterprise and innovation' which can be said to exist separately from efficient management even in the large corporation. It is a reward for the temporary monopoly gained by the successful innovator who succeeds for a time in being ahead of the rest of the business pack.

The **third** view sees profit as a reward for risk taking, for the uncertainties of business decision making. In practice, this profit may often be negative but without the hope of making profits it may be considered that business owners will avoid rather than accept uncertainty and risk.

The **fourth** view is a modification of the third. It is thought to apply to the more risky activities where total long-run costs must include 'a positive profit premium to compensate for aversion to risk and coax out the supply of risk bearing (capital)'. Merchant bankers would recognise here the additional profits they seek as providers of 'venture capital'.

The **fifth** view regards profit as a 'monopoly' return which is then interpreted as a return to a 'contrived or artificial scarcity'. This appears to be the view adopted by many school textbook writers who then link it with the rather emotive and disparaging term 'abnormal profit', a term, incidentally, that Samuelson avoids.

The **sixth** view recognises the Marxian interpretation of profit as *surplus value* – wealth created by economic activity but denied to the worker by the owners of capital. This last view opens up further problems and controversies which are beyond the scope of this book.

Samuelson's careful analysis of the different elements contained in profit is clearly more accurate and realistic than the over simple, but confusing distinction between 'normal' and 'abnormal', 'super-normal' or 'pure profit' commonly taught at the introductory levels of study. We have, therefore, avoided these terms in the computer exercises but recognised their widespread use in the chapter presentation. We hope, however, that this note will encourage teachers and students to give the problem more thought. We also hope that it will help to overcome some of the prejudice against profit-seeking economic enterprise that such terms as 'abnormal' may appear to foster.

9

Imperfect Competition

Monopolistic Competition

Features of Monopolistic Competition

Between the extremes of perfect competition and pure monopoly there exists imperfect competition. One possibility is that a market may have some elements of perfect competition and some of monopoly. Not surprisingly this has been termed **monopolistic competition**.

Such a market is said to exist when there are many competing suppliers of essentially similar products but each supplier has succeeded in differentiating his own product to some extent. The following conditions are, therefore, necessary for this market structure:

1 The products are similar but not homogeneous. Customers perceive a difference and express preferences for the goods of particular suppliers. This tendency is likely to be encouraged by suppliers through advertising, through emphasising relatively minor or superficial distinctions, often just of packaging, appearance or presentation, and by developing distinctive brand images with the implication that each brand has unique features. Clearly, a supplier is a monopolist in the supply of his own particular brands.

2 No buyers, or groups of buyers acting together, must be in a position to influence price by their actions alone and although buyers perceive differences between the products of different suppliers they regard these as close substitutes. Price differences are only tolerated in as far as the consumer is prepared to pay extra for any additional feature offered or associated with the individual brand.

3 While a supplier has some freedom to set the price of his own brand or brands, this is very limited because it is confined to a narrow range around the market price for the class of product, and this is determined by the interaction of the market forces of supply and demand. Under monopolistic competition, it is assumed that no one supplier controls a sufficiently large share of market supply to be able to influence the market price. The supplier can be seen as a modified 'price taker' or as a severely constrained 'price maker'.

4 Communications in the market, while not perfect, are good, so that individual suppliers cannot achieve any clear technical or marketing superiority over rivals.

5 Monopolistic competition is similar to perfect competition in assuming that motivation is the search for maximum profit.

6 There is also assumed to be unrestricted entry to and exit from the market for firms and production factors. There are, therefore, no effective barriers to market entry.

The result for the individual firm in equilibrium is shown in Fig. 9.1. The situation is essentially similar to that of perfect competition except that the individual firm faces a gently sloping individual demand and average revenue curve. Monopolistic competition also assumes that firms have unrestricted entry to and exit from the market and that they all have to accept essentially similar cost conditions, i.e. no single firm has any significant technical superiority over its competitors.

The market as a whole is sufficiently competitive to produce a general market price which no individual firm is powerful enough, on its own, to alter. The individual firm can depart to some extent from this general market price for its own identifiable product by varying output.

Because the firm now has a sloping average revenue curve its marginal revenue curve is also sloping, but twice as steeply. If we assume an

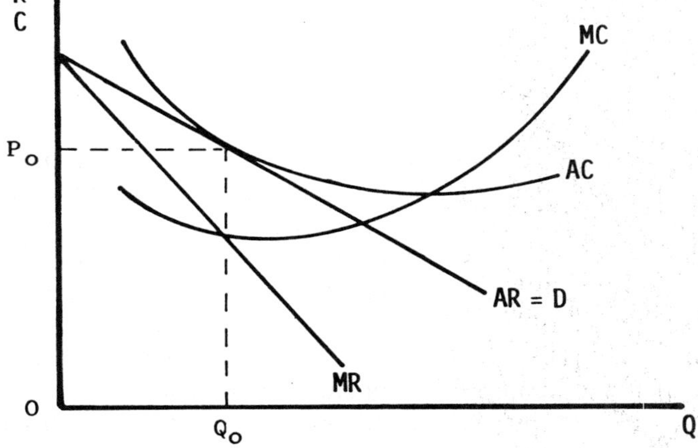

Fig. 9.1 Monopolistic competition in equilibrium
Profit maximisation is a survival condition. No super-normal profits are possible. At the profit maximising output Q_0 the average cost curve is still falling so that the firm is not producing at the lowest possible resource cost.

objective of profit maximisation, the firm produces at output Q_0 and charges the market clearing price of P_0. If, at this price the firm is able to make super-normal profits as defined in Chapter 8, so too will other firms. Under monopolistic competition, the individual firm's experience is common to its competitors. The existence of these profits will attract additional supply and this increase in market supply will tend to reduce the market price.

If the market supply continues to increase, the price may fall below the level at which even normal profits can be made and firms will start to leave the market.

As with perfect competition, these are conditions of disequilibrium. The market can only achieve supply equilibrium if there is no incentive for firms to enter or leave the market. This is reached when super-normal profit is eliminated and the average cost curve is at a tangent to the firm's average revenue curve. This is the position reached in Fig. 9.1.

The equilibrium price is P_0 at quantity level Q_0. As with perfect competition the profit maximising price is a market survival price. At any price below the average cost curve the firm cannot achieve the minimum profit needed to survive in the market.

In monopolistic competition, the firm has achieved some small measure of influence over demand and price but not enough to free it from dependence on market price nor to enable it to achieve supernormal profits and technical superiority over competitors. Prices are still likely to fluctuate in response to shifts in demand. It is not a comfortable market for suppliers who will be seeking increased market power.

Oligopoly

The Oligopolistic Market

Oligopoly is the name given to those markets where supply is controlled by relatively few firms – few, that is, in relation to the size of the market so that any increase in sales by one firm has an effect on sales of other suppliers. There is, therefore, a high degree of interdependence between oligopolists. In the UK by 1980, oligopoly had become the most common structure for national markets in manufactured goods and was becoming more prevalent in the main service industries, including the financial services. The more competitive economic conditions for the early 1980s, the rise of a group of 'newly industrialised countries', especially those in the Far East and increasing Government and banking support for small enterprises, might have been expected to have weakened some of the oligopolies. There is little evidence of this, however, and some sectors, such as retailing and building societies have become rather more oligopolistic.

This trend has continued in spite of official attempts to control and limit it. Public policy and legislation usually refer to 'monopolies' although it is now widely recognised that a more accurate description is 'oligopoly'. Nevertheless, it must also be recognised that anti-monopoly (oligopoly) or 'anti-trust' – the American term – policies in most countries, including the UK, have been remarkably ineffective. One reason for this failure is that modern economic theory contains no generally accepted model of oligopoly capable of anything like a full explanation of the main implications of this market structure. There are models which explain certain aspects of behaviour and there are many theories and controversies, but there is no single oligopoly model in the sense of the widely accepted concept of perfect competition.

Measures of Oligopoly

An indication of the strength of an oligopoly is given by measuring the extent to which total supply to a given market is **concentrated** in the hands of a limited number of firms. One measure is called the market **concentration ratio**. Thus, a 5 firm concentration ratio of 80 would indicate that 80% (four fifths) of the home market supply was provided by the largest five domestic firms in that particular industry.

Official British figures are published of these 5 firm ratios and these do show that oligopolistic markets exist in most sectors of the economy. These measures do not, unfortunately, indicate the extent and consequences of foreign imports, nor do they show the effect of what is called 'vertical monopoly'. This occurs when the market for a product is owned or under the control of an important input market or retail outlet. For example, competition between manufacturers of confectionery is limited because the two main ingredient markets of confectionery, flour and sugar, are both highly concentrated.

There are several other measures of concentration and these all have important uses. They also have their defects so that a single, comprehensive measure of oligopoly has not yet been developed. What these problems do suggest is that our understanding of oligoply may be broadened if we look not just at the market in general but also at the structure and behaviour of the individual firm. After all, we are here concerned with large, often very large, business organisations. These are likely to have considerable freedom to establish their own price and output levels. If, then, we focus our analysis on the firm, we can hope to gain a better view of the really important market features such as prices, output and the use of capital and labour.

Objectives of the Firm

Managerial Power

If firms are operating under conditions which approach those of perfect competition, we do not have to be too concerned with the objectives of the firm because these are constrained by the conditions of the market. We have shown earlier that profit maximisation is a condition of survival in this market. The successful survivors of perfect competition will be profit maximisers whether or not this was their intention.

In oligopolistic markets, however, firms have a choice. If we assume that a large oligopolist can operate under conditions similar to those of the monopolist and can make supernormal profits as indicated in Fig. 8.4, then this firm can choose any output level between the two break-even points, Q_3 and Q_2. These are the output levels where average cost is just equal to average revenue so that revenue just 'breaks even' with cost which we can assume includes an element of 'normal profit' (see Appendix to Chapter 8) sufficient to keep the firm in the market. Similarly it can choose any price level between P_3 and P_2. It does not **have to** profit maximise. This freedom from the need for profit maximisation allows it to pursue other objectives.

If we now consider the nature of the large, modern business organisation we can also see that the pursuit of objectives other than profit maximisation, becomes a real possibility. Many observers have argued that the shareholders of the large business corporation have lost control and that effective power has passed to the professional managers who are able to pursue their own aims.

This proposition is usually referred to as the 'divorce of ownership and control'. Not everyone agrees that such divorce is widespread and we also need to remember that in recent years powerful new shareholders have emerged in the form of pension funds and other 'financial institutions'. We cannot here become too involved in this controversy but by now you will have realised that there are many important issues related to the study of oligopoly.

Revenue Maximisation

Several theories exist concerning the nature of these aims. All include profit in some form or other but we must remember that the pursuit of profit **together with** other objectives is a very different matter from **profit maximisation**. There are quite distinct output, price, cost and even investment implications which follow from an assumption of profit maximisation and which have to be considerably modified once we abandon the search for the best possible profit as a sole business aim.

One American economist, Baumol has suggested a simple alternative to profit maximisation. Assuming that the large firm was 'managerially controlled' he argued that it was more likely to seek to **maximise revenue** once a certain minimum profit had been achieved. The minimum profit was necessary to satisfy the shareholders and institutions of the finance markets whose goodwill was needed when the firm sought to obtain investment funds. Once the minimum profit had been gained, Baumol argued that managers sought to achieve the highest possible level of sales revenue and that they were prepared to sacrifice some profit in the pursuit of revenue. Baumol regarded revenue as being important to managers because very often managerial prestige and salary was dependent upon it rather than upon profit. His theory simply replaces shareholder self-interest by managerial self-interest.

If you refer once more to Fig. 8.4 you can see the effect on the output and price levels when an objective of profit maximisation is replaced by revenue maximisation.

The output and price levels necessary to achieve the highest possible **profit** are Q_0 and P_0 respectively. Those needed to produce the highest possible **revenue** are Q_1 and P_1. The revenue maximising output is that level where marginal revenue is equal to zero. If you cannot see why, you should revise Chapter 7. Can you also remember the value of price elasticity of demand when $MR = 0$ and when total revenue is at its maximum?

Must the revenue maximising output always be greater than that needed for maximum profit? For the two to be the same it would be necessary for $MR = MC = 0$; i.e. for marginal cost to be zero. This is perhaps just possible at certain crucial output levels where some economies of scale, e.g. of large scale purchasing, were becoming significant. It is, however, rather unlikely. There are always likely to be some input costs resulting from an increase in output. If, then we assume that $MC>0$ we can also assume that the revenue maximising firm will tend to produce a higher output at a lower price than if it were seeking the largest possible profit.

There is, of course one qualification we need to make. The firm has to achieve a **minimum level of profit** before the managers are free to concentrate on sales revenue. The harder it becomes to achieve this minumum profit the closer behaviour will approach to profit maximisation. If actual profits fall below the minimum level then the recovery of profit and the pressure to achieve maximum profits will replace all other objectives.

When the 'managerial theories of the firm' were being developed in the 1950s and 1960s most of the world's industrial economies were growing and successful and writers were able to assume that the large oligopolistic firms were able to make profits without difficulty. In the much harsher and more competitive conditions of the 1980s, this assumption can no longer be made. It is interesting to note that many of the largest manufacturing groups in Britain and the USA, responded to the changed conditions by reducing their size. They sold subsidiary companies, dropped out of their less profitable markets and ceased to produce their less profitable products. This reaction suggests that expansion had been allowed to proceed at the expense of profit in the earlier period.

Other Theories of the Firm

Revenue maximisation is probably the simplest of the theories offered as a replacement for profit maximisation. Other writers have argued that growth, which is not necessarily the same as the pursuit of sales revenue, is a powerful objective and will be pursued at the expense of profit as long as this does not threaten the safety of the firm (and the ruling managerial team), perhaps by allowing the share price to fall to the extent that takeover becomes possible.

Some writers have suggested that managers may be influenced by several objectives so that no single objective can ever be 'maximised'. In their view, managers seek a **satisfactory** level of achievement. The firm's behaviour is then said to be **satisficing** rather than maximising or optimising. It is difficult to find a replacement for this rather ugly term and it has to be admitted that many decisions of large firms that are hard to explain on the basis of traditional economic theories, do fit 'satisficing' explanations.

Oligopolistic Collusion

It will now be apparent that there is a great deal of controversy surrounding the whole subject of oligopoly and it is not possible to put forward a single, generally accepted model of this type of market. Nevertheless, there are some aspects of behaviour that can be deduced from most of the main theories and one of these is the tendency for oligopolists to collude, i.e. to follow very similar policies and patterns of behaviour. Most formal agreements between firms over such matters as prices, payments to distributors and other practices which limit competition are now banned in the USA and Europe by anti-trust, fair-trading or competition laws and EEC regulations. Few of these laws seem to have had much effect on oligopolistic competition. The harsh economic climate of the early 1980s probably did more to increase genuine business competition than all the legislation of the previous 30 years.

Some of the earliest attempts to analyse oligopolistic markets were able to show that firms could increase profits by entering into market sharing agreements instead of competing with each other. Formal collusion, or simply refraining from competition, would permit each firm to charge higher prices and make more profit. Some modern theories of behaviour have indicated that a powerful influence on firms is the desire to avoid, or reduce, uncertainty. Competition increases uncertainty and is, therefore, avoided or kept within certain well-established limits. Common sense also suggests that if large firms, using similar technology, are offering very similar products to the same market, any attempt by one to reduce price will be followed by the others so that all are left with unchanged shares of total market sales but with reduced revenues and profits from those sales. Similarly, any attempt to compete by increased advertising or by offering larger discounts to the retail stores will also be followed by similar action from the other firms. Again, all will suffer increased costs and reduced profits.

We are left to draw the conclusion that collusion rather than competition is the most likely pattern of behaviour to be expected from an oligopolistic market structure. Existing large firms are more likely to seek expansion by producing new products or by taking over weaker firms in new markets than by competing with other large and well-established firms.

Possible benefits from collusion can be illustrated by the following very simple model of a market in which there are two suppliers only. This is called a **duopoly**.

Suppose the two suppliers in this market are Uniwash and Dazzlewhite. Each firm markets a washing powder of similar quality. Their market research indicates that a 'jumbo' packet of the powder can be sold at prices of £1 or £1.50. Dazzlewhite believes that the possible profit it can achieve by selling the powder at these prices is represented by the following matrix:

		Uniwash	
	Price	**£1**	**£1.50**
Dazzlewhite	**£1**	95	120
	£1.50	85	110

Thus, if Dazzlewhite charges £1 and Uniwash also charges £1 then profit is 95. If Dazzlewhite charges £1.50 and Uniwash charges £1 then profit falls to 85.

For its part Uniwash believes that its profit matrix is:

		Uniwash	
	Price	**£1**	**£1.50**
Dazzlewhite	**£1**	95	85
	£1.50	120	110

Thus, if Uniwash charges £1 and Dazzlewhite charges £1 then its profit is 95, but if it charges £1.50 and Dazzlewhite charges £1 then the profit falls to 85.

A close look at these two matrices suggests that, left to themselves, the safest strategy for each firm to adopt is to charge £1 so that each obtains 95 profit. However, if the firms collude and each agree to charge £1.50 then each can raise profit to 110. At the same time, we see that each firm may be tempted to break the agreement secretly. Even bigger profits of 120 are available if there is a secret price reduction to £1 while the other firm stays at £1.50. It is, of course, unlikely that secret price reductions will remain secret for very long. Awareness of probable early discovery is likely to keep the collusive pact in force. Nevertheless, this simple model does show the inherent instability of oligopolistic collusion.

Notice that almost any discussion of oligopoly obliges us to make assumptions about the behaviour and objectives of the oligopolistic firms. It is the firm, therefore, that tends to become the focus of attention and when we take this into account the absence of any general model of oligopoly appears less significant.

At the same time it must also be recognised that the majority of markets for goods and services in the United Kingdom have now become oligopolistic and highly concentrated, in the sense that a high proportion of the output supplied to a market is accounted for by a relatively few firms. Large numbers of industries in the advanced industrial countries can now fairly be described as oligopolistic and many are dominated by a very small number of large firms whose decisions affect the fortunes of countless smaller, dependent firms. This gives an added importance to the questions surrounding the behaviour and objectives of large firms, a topic introduced in Chapter 4. In an oligopoly the behaviour of the firm is essentially the same as the behaviour of the industry. It is not surprising, therefore, that modern analysis in industrial economics pays considerable attention to the objectives, behaviour and performance of the individual large firm.

In Britain, official figures are issued for the concentration ratios of industries based on the five largest firms in each industry. Thus, if the five largest firms account for 60% of output then the concentration ratio is 60 (also shown sometimes as 0.6). Some actual concentration ratios are shown in the Appendix at the end of this chapter.

Exercises Relating to Chapter 9

1 Explain why it is possible for an oligopolist to pursue business objectives other than profit maximisation.

2 An advertisement for a type of bread was once based on the slogan 'Don't say Brown say Hovis'. Explain the objectives of this campaign with the help of economic analysis.

3 What forms can business collusion take? Why may oligopolists collude? Why are collusive agreements sometimes unstable?

4 From the published reports and accounts obtained for question 5 in Chapter 4 obtain details of the structure of share ownership for the companies. How far do these figures support the argument that there is a divorce between the control and ownership of large public companies?

5 Identify one industry in which large firms predominate and another in which there are many small firms. Discuss as fully as possible the reasons for the difference.

Appendix: Concentration Levels in selected United Kingdom Industries

The following figures are based on the Census of Production 1983 and relate to **Enterprises**. (An enterprise can be defined as a business firm or group of firms which operates a single undertaking even though it may contain many different companies and organisations and operate from many locations.)

Industry	*Number in industry*	*% held by 5 largest of* Sales	Employment
Sugar and sugar by-products	12	100	100
Man made fibres	20	93	93
Cement, lime, plaster	58	91	92
Motor vehicles and their engines	187	91	88
Aerospace equipment manufacturing and rep.	312	79	71
Chemical industry	827	59	53
Glass, glassware	567	48	55
Non-ferrous metal	591	44	44
Extraction of stone, clay, sand, and gravel	497	39	36
Printing and publishing	10210	21	19
Bolts, nuts, washers, rivets, springs and non-precision chains	1485	15	13

These measures have serious limitations. They relate to production in the United Kingdom only and they usually define the industry in strictly production terms, taking no account of product choice as perceived by the buyer. Consider, for example, the product choices open to a person considering possible coverings for a kitchen floor. To attempt, therefore, to measure market power simply in these terms can give a distorted picture. Imported goods, for example, are a major force in many markets including motor vehicles and many items of household equipment. The whole concept of the market area is likely to change as a result of the removal of national trade barriers within the European Community in 1992.

Nevertheless, despite all their limitations, measures of concentration relating to clearly defined industries are still useful and provide an essential starting point for study of market power and business competition.

10

Competition and rivalry in imperfect markets

Business Attitudes to Competition

It is often assumed that economists are suspicious of monopoly and tend to favour markets that approximate to perfect competition. This assumption and the development of public policies towards competition are examined more closely in Chapter 11. At this stage we take a closer look at competition.

Competitive markets are not always welcomed by those who have to operate in them. Business management has been described as the process of taking decisions under conditions of uncertainty. The greater the degree of uncertainty the more difficult it is to make correct decisions. Competition increases the uncertainty of the environment within which any business manager operates and, therefore, decision making becomes more hazardous and the results are more difficult to predict. Consequently, we can expect business managers to try to reduce this element of uncertainty by restricting market competition.

When we examine highly concentrated business markets our interest extends to two important aspects of business behaviour:

a The way in which firms already established in a market seek to limit entry by possible new competitors.

b The way established firms behave towards each other in coping with market conditions where there is no effective price competition, but where there remains a considerable degree of business rivalry between suppliers in the efforts to maintain or achieve market domination, to secure brand leadership or to ensure that they are not taken by surprise by the actions of their rival oligopolists in the market.

Actions to Prevent the Entry of New Competitors.

These actions are likely to involve both pricing and non-pricing strategies.

Limit Pricing

This suggests that firms are able to set prices at levels which effectively discourage the entry of competitors. A model can be developed to illustrate this issue. It assumes that:

1 Established firms enjoy cost advantages denied to most new entrants. Such cost advantages are likely to arise out of well-established production processes, efficient production teams, economies of large scale production, close connections with distributors and brand images that have gained widespread acceptance from buyers.

2 Established firms will continue to produce at pre-entry quantity levels after entry by a new competitor. This is usually known as the Sylos postulate after the economist who first drew attention to the tendency and analysed its implications. Should new entrants, able to achieve the minimum efficient size of output and the long run cost curves of established firms, come into the market total market supply will rise and the market price will fall.

The consequences of this assumption are shown in Fig. 10.1.
If established firms charge prices above P_0 they risk entry. If they charge below P_1 they sacrifice profit. There is thus a trade-off between achieving current stability with the chance of maintaining satisfactory long-term profits, and increasing short-term profits but with greater risk of entry. Firms able to choose between these alternatives are likely to be influenced by the ease of entry to the market by new firms. This is now often known as the extent to which markets are contestable and contestability depends on such influences as the production methods involved, e.g. the size of capital investment required to start production, the size of the potential market and the stage reached in the product's normal life cycle – entry is easier in growing markets than in those which have reached saturation levels – the profitability of the established firms and the degree of customer and distributor satisfaction with existing products.

Predatory Pricing

The limit pricing model assumes that firms do not change their behaviour in the face of the threat of entry in the belief that their current practices are an effective deterrent. The predatory pricing model assumes that firms do react strongly to the possibility of challenge from outside the market.

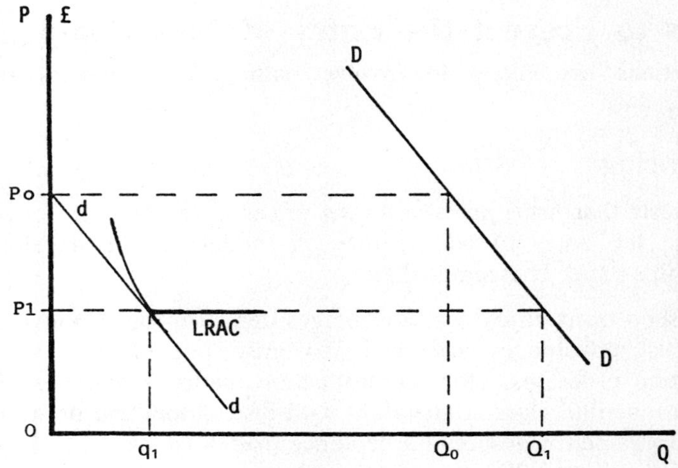

Fig. 10.1 This is based on entry barriers resulting from economies of scale, the most commonly assumed case. Quantity q_1 is the minimum efficient scale of production. Entry is only considered by firms able to produce at this level. The long-run average cost curve is common to all firms. D is market demand and established firms are expected to maintain output after entry. Thus, established firms produce output Q_0. A new entrant adds output q_1 which increases market supply to Q_1 ($Q_1 - Q_0 = q_1$). Post entry price would fall to P_1 and this effectively discourages entry. P_0 is, therefore, the price limit.

A new entrant can be forced out of a market by the practice of charging very low prices, even at the cost of the established firms having to suffer losses. Established firms are likely to be strong enough to do this and have strong enough profit reserves to stand the losses for a limited period. They may also be able to subsidise losses from profits from other, unthreatened product sectors. When the new entrant has been forced to withdraw, the established firms can usually raise prices and restore profits.

Predatory pricing is also associated with the behaviour of dominant firms which feel that they are strong enough to establish a greater degree of monopoly power by forcing out rivals whose practices they dislike. This kind of behaviour is more likely to be associated with a market in transition than with an established and high concentrated oligopoly.

Defensive Advertising

Advertising, particularly when combined with multiple branding (marketing what is essentially the same product under several different and apparently competing brand names) can be a barrier to competition. When there are no serious technical or production cost barriers to entry of new firms to a market, one way to discourage entry is to raise the costs and reduce the potential rewards of entry. If there were only two brands of domestic washing powder – one from each of the two firms dominating this market – any new firm offering a third would quickly gain a substantial market share simply by offering some variety to bored consumers. In fact there are many brands, some of which are constantly supported by very substantial advertising. A firm considering entry to this market would have to spend heavily to match this advertising and could hope to gain a much smaller share because there appears to be a wide choice of brands, some of which are held in reserve to be re-launched as 'new' if serious competition is anticipated.

Signals to Potential Entrants that Entry Will Be Resisted

Any potential entrants will consider the probability of successful entry, the costs of entry and the subsequent gains to be made. All the entry-limiting techniques so far considered are designed to raise its costs and reduce its potential rewards. It is also possible for existing suppliers to signal that they have committed substantial resources to the market and will not, therefore, withdraw without a fierce fight. Signals of this kind may include:

a Building up over capacity so that entry can be resisted by flooding the market and driving down the product price.
b Acquiring highly specialised machinery with no opportunity cost outside this particular market. The need to defend these 'sunk costs' indicates determination to remain in that market.
c A past record of successful resistance to entry attempts and statements from senior executives that entry will be resisted.

Behaviour Towards Oligopolistic Rivals

One of the contributions of the so-called Austrian school of economists has been to show that competitive behaviour still exists, even within markets which economists have not traditionally recognised as competitive. This behaviour may have as its main purpose the achievement of greater security, prestige or income for managers. Nevertheless, as the 'Austrian school' has argued, the end result is often to produce new or improved products, to raise the standard of service, to introduce new methods of distribution and marketing and generally to bring benefits to consumers. One of the most important objectives of any marketing strategy is to achieve brand leadership, i.e. for the market to recognise that a particular brand has the largest market share. Achieving this objective brings substantial practical benefits. These include access to buyers in the distributive trades, allocation of adequate shelf space within stores and ability to claim the more attractive shelf and display locations in stores. New brand promotions from existing brand leader producers are also likely to be taken seriously by store buyers. Precisely because brand leadership is so desirable, existing brands are seldom allowed to retain their position without constant challenge from rival brands. It is, therefore, against this background of competing for the favour of the buyer that we should view the behaviour of firms in oligopolistic markets.

Market Segmentation

Rather than compete over a very wide front, firms frequently seek to achieve dominance in particular sectors of the market. Before market conditions were transformed by electronics, information technology and the entry of powerful foreign suppliers, the British market for weighing machines was divided into two. One firm dominated the supply of domestic weighing machines (mostly kitchen and bathroom scales) and rarely strayed into the production of equipment for business organisations. Another firm made virtually no domestic scales but dominated the supply of weighing equipment to business firms. Dividing the market in this way allows suppliers to achieve a degree of monopoly power in their particular sector while, at the same time, retaining the capability of challenging suppliers in neighbouring sectors should circumstances suggest that this would be possible and profitable. Sometimes geographical segmentation is practised. Although common practice in the personal services, for consumer goods this is more likely to be found in international markets than in relatively small national markets such as those of Great Britain. You should be alert for evidence of this reaction to what some business managers might perceive as the 'threat' of increased competition and loss of market domination in the wider European markets promised for 1992.

Product Differentiation

This is similar in many ways to market segmentation and may be closely associated with it. The idea of product differentiation is to produce a full range of product brands so that all tastes and needs in the market are provided for, with no obvious gaps to tempt possible new entrants nor to provide opportunities for rivals to increase their total market share. One interesting and slightly puzzling feature of the practice is that particular product types tend to become associated with particular suppliers and attempts by rivals to challenge successful and established brands by very close substitutes are rarely successful. Developments in the British confectionery industry in 1988 suggest that it is easier to take over a long established manufacturing company than to launch new brands to challenge its market leadership.

Advertising

As already indicated, heavy advertising can be a form of defence against entry but it is also a very powerful tool for establishing brand images and loyalty and for seeking to secure a significant, if not dominant, market share. Some observers suggest that it gives the illusion of competition where none really exists but it can also be seen as a very important form of rivalry whereby suppliers compete for the favour of consumers and which helps to establish the reality of consumer sovereignty. Distributors clearly think that product advertising is important and large national store chains may refuse shelf space to new brands unless they receive an assurance that the brand will be supported by a guaranteed volume of advertising. When most brands were manufacturer brands, relatively few retail companies engaged in large scale consumer advertising. With the growth of retailer 'own brands' the volume of retailer advertising has been increasing. Branding and advertising clearly go closely together.

Mergers

This is an aspect of oligopolistic behaviour that cannot be ignored. It is the ultimate defence against competition and market rivalry. Some economists suggest that pressures to merge increased side by side with government hostility and action against trade collusion (restrictive trade practices). However, mergers are a major element in public policy towards competition and they are examined more fully in the next chapter.

Price Discrimination

The greater the degree of market power achieved by suppliers, the greater their ability to take advantage of differing demand characteristics in differing segments of the total product market. Price discrimination is the term used to describe the practice of charging different prices for what is essentially the same product according to different groups of buyers. It is, therefore, a rather special form of market segmentation.

When Price Discrimination is possible

Price discrimination is possible when a firm or group of firms acting together can control supply to the extent that they can prevent buyers at low prices re-entering the market as competing sellers, and also avoid resentment from those buyers who are unable to obtain preferential prices. Some degree of monopoly power is thus essential for the practice of price discrimination.

The possibility of charging discriminatory prices arises because people have differing marginal utilities for any particular product and because they are influenced to differing degrees by the various factors that affect demand. Thus, some people are more influenced by price than others and successful price discrimination is very much a matter of exploiting differences in marginal utilities and in price elasticities of demand.

Degrees of Price Discrimination

Economists usually distinguish three degrees of Discrimination.

1 *First Degree or Perfect Discrimination*
The most complete or perfect degree is sought through haggling, whereby the seller seeks to charge each customer the highest price he or she is prepared to pay, i.e. up to each customer's marginal utility. Suppose a seller has ten possible customers for a product, each with a different valuation of marginal utility. Together this group makes up what is effectively the demand curve for the product shown in Fig. 10.2.

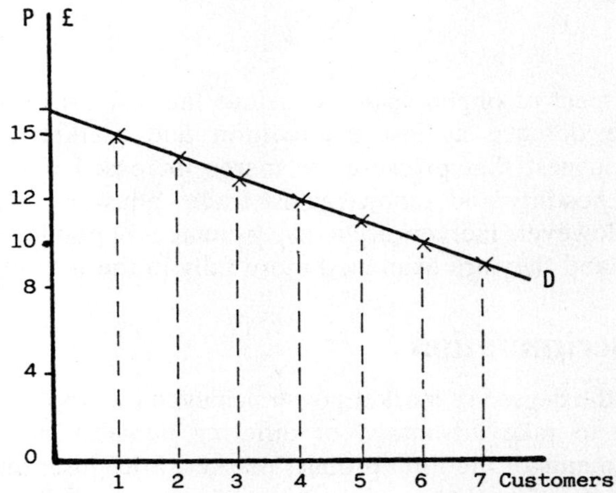

Fig. 10.2 If successful haggling achieves sales to each customer at a price equal to the value of the customer's marginal utility, total revenue is greater than can be achieved at any single price between £10 and £15.

One customer is prepared to pay £15, the second £14, the third £13 and so on. If the seller is prepared to sell at any price down to £10, but not below £10 then bargaining can take place to try to obtain the maximum from each buyer. Success would produce a total revenue of £75 £(15+14+13+12+11+10) which is higher than can be obtained by selling all at any single price on the market demand curve (6 × £10 = £60). Individual haggling can be very effective, provided the seller is more skilled than the buyer and provided it does not raise costs above the additional revenue it produces. Success usually depends on the seller having a financial stake in the bargaining process. It is not a suitable practice for large-scale retailing in which relatively unskilled assistants are employed.

2 *Second Degree Discrimination*
This practice occurs when the seller does not attempt to achieve a large number of individual prices but is prepared to offer price concessions to selected customers or groups of customers with a special market power. For genuine discrimination to exist, the price reduction must be greater than can be justified on the grounds of large scale buying and must not be freely offered to any buyer prepared to meet bulk order conditions. A possible situation is illustrated in Fig. 10.3 where the supplier's preferred price is P_0 at which price Q_0 units can be sold. This is the price charged generally but favoured customers are allowed to pay P_1 and the additional sales at this reduced price increase total revenue to $(P_0Q_0) + P_1(Q_1-Q_0)$.

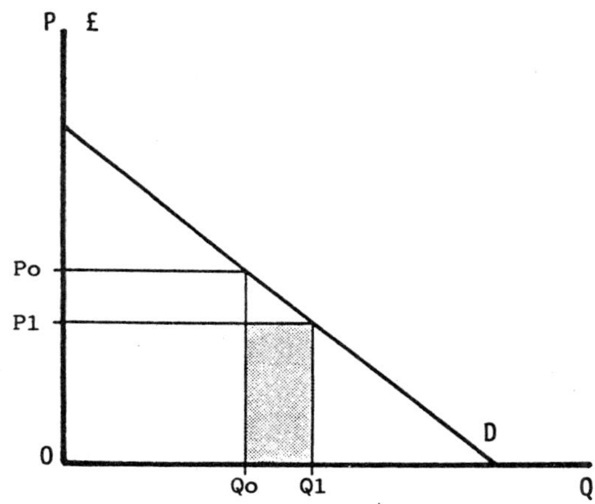

Fig. 10.3 The normal price is P_0 achieving total revenue equal to $P_0 \times Q_0$. Certain favoured customers are charged price P_1 to achieve additional revenue equal to the shaded area.

3 *Third Degree Discrimination*
This occurs when the seller is able to identify two or more distinct markets with differing price elasticities of demand at the range of prices within which sales are permitted.

This is illustrated in Fig. 10.4 which shows two separate markets (A and B) and the combined market (A + B). For simplicity it is assumed that the practice makes no difference to costs so that the cost (C_0) is the same whether discrimination takes place or not. Consequently, the MC curve shows the costs of producing for either market. If the firm tries to

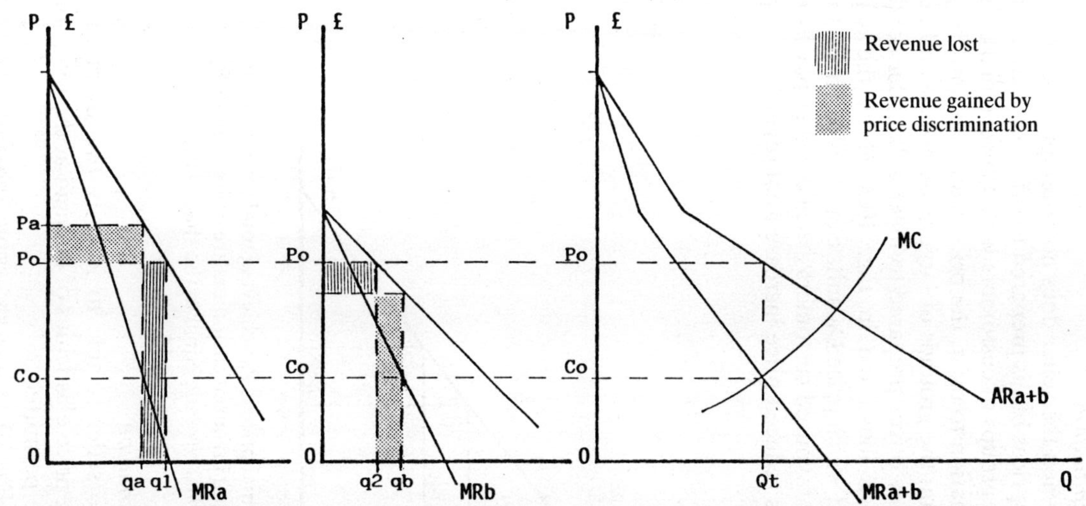

Fig. 10.4 Without price discrimination the common market price is P_0 and the total quantity sold to the market is Q. Assuming costs remain unchanged, price discrimination does not change the total quantity sold but the price rise in market A is greater than the price fall in market B. The total revenue gain is greater than the total revenue loss. As costs are unchanged, profits rise. This model also assumes profit maximisation as an objective.

maximise profit it can increase its profits by discriminatory pricing rather than setting a uniform price for all buyers.

If the firm sets a uniform price it will produce at an output level at which marginal cost (MC) = aggregate marginal revenue (MR a + b). The aggregate MR curve is derived by aggregating the individual market marginal revenue curves. Effectively, the firm allocates output to the market which offers the highest marginal revenue. The firm will set the uniform price P_0 which clears total market demand with total sales of Q. This total is allocated by selling q_1 in market A and q_2 in market B.

The firm could increase its profits by setting different prices in each market. It does this by equating the marginal revenue in each market with the marginal cost (C_0) at the profit maximising output level of Q. In market A the firm will sell qa and in market B sales are qb. The respective market clearing prices in each market are Pa and Pb.

This results in the price rising in the market where demand is less price-elastic (A) and falling in the market where the price elasticity is higher (B). Total quantity sold does not change. The reduced quantity in A is exactly matched by the increased quantity in B. Because, however, the price rise in A is greater than the fall in B total revenue rises. As costs are unchanged this means that total profit is greater if price discrimination is practised. To summarise, price discrimination is possible if:

1 The firm has significant monopoly power.
2 It is possible to identify and keep separate at least two distinct markets.
3 In the region of the profit maximising uniform price, the price elasticity of demand in each separate market is different.

The Special Case of Spare Capacity

There is a further form of price discrimination which can be recognised. This is the decision to charge a special price to gain an additional order when the firm has spare production capacity.

Firms frequently find that they are able to supply their 'normal' orders and still have machine and labour time that could be more fully used. They usually know the average cost of production at their normal output levels and they may refuse to accept any additional orders unless these can be met at a price that covers the average cost and the expected amount of profit. This refusal could be mistaken. Consider the following example:

Firm A produces 'winklets' with the following cost pattern. (Its normal production is 50 000 units per month.)

	£
Fixed costs	10 000
Variable costs	
£1 per unit so	
50 000@ £1	50 000
Total cost	60 000

Cost per unit is £60 000 ÷ 50 000 = £1.20
The firm's normal practice is to add on 25% for profit so price is the average (unit) cost + £0.30 giving a unit price of £1.50
Total revenue, assuming the normal month's production is sold at the desired price, is:

	£
50 000 @ £1.50	75 000
Less total cost	60 000
Profit for month	15 000

Suppose, the firm is offered an additional contract to supply 10 000 units at a price of £1.10. The manager turns down the order because it would represent a loss. Was the manager right?
The answer depends on whether the order can be produced without any increase in fixed costs. If there is spare capacity then the firm should be able to do so. If it can, then the firm's new cost pattern is as follows:

	£	
Fixed costs	10 000	
Variable costs	60 000	(60 000 @ £1)
Total cost	70 000	

Total revenue at the offer price added to the existing orders

	£
50 000 @ £1.60	75 000
10 000 @ £1.10	11 000
Total revenue	86 000
Less total cost	70 000
Month's profit	16 000

The profit would be £1000 higher with the order even though this is at a price less than the average total cost. Under these conditions, therefore, and provided there is no possibility of re-sale to any of the existing customers or of complaints from existing customers, then the order should be accepted. We could also argue that the additional order would enable a slight price reduction to be made to existing customers if it could be priced at anything above £1.17 – the new average total cost at the higher output of 60 000 units. At a price lower than this no price reduction could be justified as the order would not be contributing its full share of fixed costs.

The argument that profit will be increased if a price above average variable cost can be obtained is really making use of the concept of opportunity cost. The opportunity cost of using spare capacity of machines or people is nothing and need not, therefore, be added to the cost of increasing production.

If, of course, the manager judged that there was a danger that existing customers would be upset and demand price reductions if they were to hear of the low-priced order, then the refusal would be justified. Price discrimination can only benefit the supplier if customers can be kept fully separate and there is no possibility of losing existing business as a result of discrimination.

Instability in Oligopolies

Within established oligopolistic markets the behaviour of individual firms can be assumed to have three main objectives. These are:

1 To exploit market power in order to increase profits. At this stage of study an objective of profit maximisation is generally assumed but in Chapters 4 and 9 the possibility is raised that other, more specifically managerial, objectives may be pursued. If the group controlling the firm's major decisions is, in fact, pursuing another goal such as growth, then market power is likely to be used to further this.
2 To achieve a satisfactory way of living with existing rivals in the market. All models of oligopoly indicate that continuous all-out price or non-price competition can only lead to falling profits and, in many cases, to escalating costs. It also creates an unacceptable degree of uncertainty for managerial decision making. In business, as in politics, continuous all-out conflict is unrealistic. Participants have to establish formal or informal rules in order to live together. Political conflict is regulated by conventions and understandings. It may seem strange that politicians who understand this method of living with conflict find it intolerable in business where similar behaviour is condemned as collusion. On the other hand, consumers can suffer from unrestricted business collusion. Clearly, there is a very thin line between behaviour that is an acceptable method of restraining destructive conflict and that which damages the economy through undue restrictions on competition.
3 To prevent entry to the market by new competitors. This is one of the aspects of oligopolistic behaviour which most concerns economists. One of the most serious effects of successfully limiting entry for a long period

is that established firms lose the habit of competing and they can quickly lose ground if powerful competitors do gain entry.

No oligopoly is completely secure in the long run, though some do survive for very long periods. Collusive arrangements, however, are often insecure. They face two constant threats. One is the temptation of established firms to cheat; this was suggested in Chapter 9. The other is that market entry will be achieved by new firms which are likely to be hostile to arrangements which increased the costs and difficulty of penetration. The most likely firms to achieve entry are those that are already large and powerful in closely associated markets, foreign firms wishing to extend their geographical boundaries and firms which achieve a genuine advance in production technology or marketing techniques that enable them to make significant reductions in unit costs. New technology, which has been too often ignored by established oligopolists resisting changes that threatened their familiar pattern of business behaviour, is probably the most powerful catalyst for changes in market structure and the nature of market competition.

The importance of superstores to consumer product distribution has made it easier for large manufacturers to jump across traditional market boundaries. Modern transport and communications and movements towards free trade, at least within the European Community, are constantly extending the geographical boundaries of markets and technological change has now become almost a normal feature of business life. All these conditions pose a threat to any established oligopoly which seeks to remain immune from developments outside its own particular market.

Actual and Potential Competition

Consideration of the ease or otherwise of entry to markets by new competitors leads to some modification of traditional views of industrial concentration and monopoly power. It is not sufficient to count the number of suppliers of a product and estimate a concentration ratio. The behaviour of existing suppliers will be as much influenced by their estimate of the danger of new competition as their need to watch the activities of their established market rivals. This, in fact, is the basis for modern economic analysis of competition using the concept of contestable markets, a concept owing much to the work of the influential American economist, W. J. Baumol who had earlier played a major part in developing the managerial theories of the firm outlined in Chapter 4 of this book.

Some of the highest levels of industrial concentration can be found in intermediate markets where components are supplied to other manufacturers. Before assuming that these must be highly uncompetitive markets, it has to be remembered that such markets may be very easy to enter, both for firms which have very similar equipment and skills to those required to produce the product and by the major buyers who have the capital resources to produce their own supplies if they believe that it is in their interests to do so. A pet food manufacturer will buy the metal cans it needs from a specialist can manufacturer only as long as this is the most cost effective method of operation. If the can supplier was suspected of abusing its apparent market power, the pet food manufacturer coud quickly establish its own can manufacturing plant. This would not only eliminate an important customer it would also produce a new competitive supplier.

It is also important to consider the nature of the market. The existing market boundaries are based on conditions as they are, not what they can quickly become following technical change. In the current state of technical knowledge a metal might be the safest and cheapest way of packaging pet food. Suppose, however, a plastic manufacturer were to produce a material which had all the advantages and qualities of metal at a fraction of the cost. Metal can manufacturers are well aware of these possibilities and they seek to avoid giving incentives to customers to become rival suppliers or to encourage potential rivals in the plastics sectors to spend money on research that might lead to further replacing metal with plastic.

These examples suggest that great care has to be taken in defining the boundaries of markets and indeed in defining the extent to which actual or potential competition does influence business behaviour. After all it is the behaviour of business firms that is the important issue. The economist seeks to know whether resources are being used efficiently, whether firms are seeking to improve efficiency through research and technological advance and whether market power is being used to the detriment of the consumer. These are the important questions, though it has to be admitted that they are less easy to define in ratio terms or to make into the foundations of statutory controls than the traditional, though now largely irrelevant, measures of monopoly power.

Exercises Relating to Chapter 10

1 Examine and discuss the nature of the entry barriers in relation to one of the following markets: fire and motor insurance; legal services; overseas tours and holidays; soaps and detergents; sugar; aircraft manufacturing; sweets, chocolate and confectionery.

2 Suggest possible future technical changes that might alter current entry conditions to your chosen market.

3 Discuss the case for and against the view that current large scale consumer product advertising is clear evidence that consumer markets are highly competitive.

4 Examine the concentration indices listed in the Appendix following Chapter 9.

How do you account for the 3 lowest and the 3 highest index figures? What further information would you seek before commenting on the degree of competition faced by the main producers in these industries?

5 In the late 1930s local bus companies in most areas issued 'workman's return' tickets at reduced prices to passengers travelling before 9 a.m. In 1988 British Rail was only prepared to issue reduced price tickets to passengers travelling outside normal work commuting times. Discuss the reasons for this change in policy towards reduced fare travelling.

11

Competition, an ideal market structure?

We have examined various aspects of the main market structures generally recognised by economists. The question naturally arises as to which of these comes closest to a market which is 'ideal' from the consumer's point of view. The usual approach is to compare the two extremes of perfect competition and monopoly and then to consider the implications for the more commonly found conditions of imperfect competition. We can start by considering the advantages of pure competition. Before doing so, however, we need to establish some concepts as a basis for analysis.

Consumer Welfare

We need, of course, to have a clear understanding of what we expect from a market. The function of any market is to allocate scarce resources so that an **ideal market** is one which achieves an **ideal pattern of resource allocation**. This would be reached if it were no longer possible to alter the pattern in any way to make one person better off without making someone else worse off. As long as it remains possible to increase the total utility of one person without reducing the utility of others then we have not reached the ideal.

Although this concept is simple enough to grasp, its application presents rather more difficulties.

Marginal Cost and Price

One approach to the problem is based on equating the marginal cost of production with the price paid by the consumer. In Chapter 5 we argued that, in equilibrium, a consumer would buy a good up to the point where his or her monetary valuation of the good, i.e. MU(money) × MU(good) = its price. If we now consider the good's market demand curve, which we can here assume to be the aggregate of all the individuals' curves, we can say something about society's valuation of the good. Each point on the curve represents the marginal consumer's valuation of the good. If the price were to rise slightly, this marginal customer would no longer be prepared to buy, because the utility to him would now be lower than the price. On the other hand, a slightly lower price would induce an additional buyer with an appropriate utility valuation to enter the market.

We can thus interpret the market demand curve as a **marginal social valuation curve**, because each point on it represents the marginal user's valuation of that good.

From the supply side of the market, the marginal cost curve represents the cost of producing each additional unit of the good for the market. The marginal cost curve is itself dependent on the prices of the raw materials and production factors used. These prices are, in turn, influenced by society's valuation of their other possible uses. The marginal cost curve may then, be interpreted as society's opportunity cost curve or as the **marginal social cost curve**.

Given the 'normal' shapes of these curves, we can depict the market situation for a possible product, say private cars, as shown in Fig. 11.1. If the total output of cars is at Q_1 the value placed by society on the last car produced is higher than that of the production uses of the resources used in its production. Society would gain by transferring resources from other uses to the manufacture of more cars.

If, however, production of private cars rose to Q2 then, at this output level, the social valuation placed on the last unit is lower than that of the other uses. Society would gain by producing fewer cars. The ideal level of private car production is at Q_0 where society places equal value on the

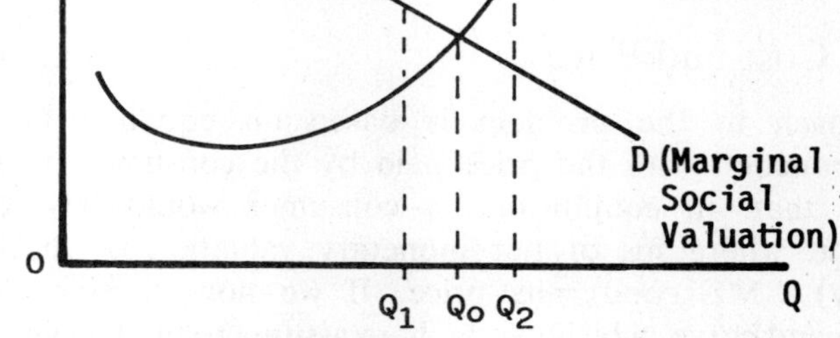

Fig. 11.1 Allocative efficiency
The demand curve can be seen as a marginal social valuation curve and the marginal cost curve as the marginal social cost curve. Only at output level Q_0 are these equal.

marginal car and on the possible alternative uses for the raw materials. This occurs where price is equal to the marginal cost of production – the cost of producing the marginal car.

If we accept this argument, we should be able to supply the same test to all products and the ideal pattern of resource distribution would be achieved when all prices were equal to all marginal production costs.

This, of course, is looking at 'efficiency' from the point of view of the allocation of goods among members of society. It is often called **allocative efficiency**. It is assumed in the discussion of allocative efficiency that goods and services are actually being produced at the lowest possible cost at the current level of technology. In practice this cannot really be assumed and there is a separate issue of **technical efficiency**. Failure on the part of a firm to achieve technical efficiency in this sense of producing each output level at the least possible cost is often called lack of **X efficiency**. Both concepts are relevant to the examination of market structures.

If you now think back over the market models examined in the past chapters, and in particular, examine Figs 8.3 and 8.4, you will recall that only **perfect competition** produces the conditions necessary for firms to produce at output levels where marginal cost is equal to market price, this being a necessary condition for long-run survival in competitive markets. This characteristic of the perfectly competitive market is a further reason for its continued attraction for economists as an ideal, in spite of its alleged remoteness from modern reality.

In each of the other market structures we have examined there is a tendency for firms to produce at output levels where price is above marginal cost, e.g. at Q_1 in Fig. 11.1, where fewer resources are devoted to a product's production than required by society's valuation.

Monopoly and Welfare Loss

Failure to achieve the position where price is equal to marginal cost, the ideal suggested earlier in this chapter, suggests that there can be a **welfare loss** resulting from a market allocation of resources. Look now at Fig. 11.2. This shows an industry which, for simplicity, we can assume has constant long-run marginal costs (LRMC). If the industry were purely competitive the equilibrium price would be P_c where no super-normal profits can be earned. At this price the area of consumer surplus received by consumers is YBP_c. If you are not sure what is meant by consumer surplus you should revise Chapter 5.

If, overnight, the industry were to be turned into a profit maximising monopoly, the price would rise to P_m and the area of consumer surplus would shrink to YAP_m. The monopolist producer, however, would enjoy super-normal profits of P_mAXP_c.

Notice that this surplus, sometimes called the **producer surplus** and

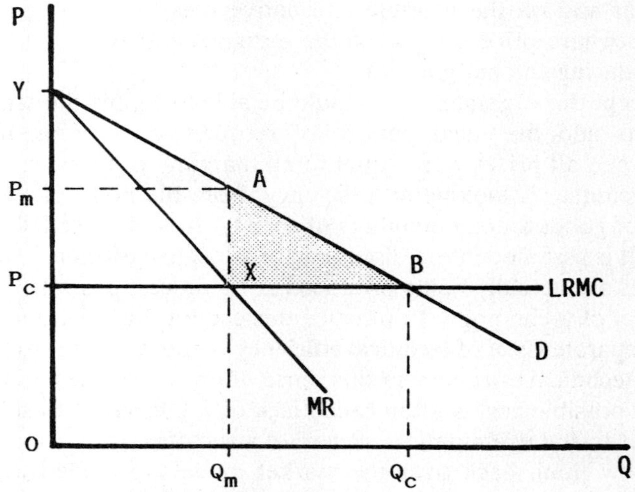

Fig. 11.2 Deadweight welfare loss
A change from perfect competition to a profit maximising monopoly would reduce output from Q_c to Q_m and raise prices from P_c to P_m. The consumer surplus shrinks to YAP_m and the producer surplus to P_mAXP_c. The area of the triangle ABX is lost to both consumer and producer and is the deadweight welfare loss.

which was previously enjoyed by the consumer, has now been transferred to the shareholders of the monopoly firm.

The area of the triangle ABX is not included in either the consumer or the producer surplus. It is lost to both and is known as the **deadweight welfare loss**.

You can test your understanding of this argument and of the difference between profit and revenue maximisation by redrawing Fig. 11.2 and by showing the changes in consumer surplus, producer surplus and deadweight welfare loss if the firm switches from a profit to a revenue maximising objective. There are also a number of questions on this topic in the computer exercises, section 7.

Changes in Efficiency

It is also often argued that competition provides incentives to increased efficiency because of the pressures on firms to produce at the least possible cost in resources. This forces them to look to new methods and new machines and to undertake genuine innovative research and develop these as rapidly as possible. Competition is thus seen as a means of reducing X inefficiency as defined earlier in this chapter.

This argument does conflict to some extent with the conditions required for perfect competition where the requirement of perfect communication would prevent any firm acquiring technical, managerial or marketing superiority over rival suppliers. It is also suggested that it is necessary to have some super-normal profit or the incentive to make such profit in order to persuade firms to undertake the risks of research and innovation.

While accepting that the extreme conditions of perfect competition might not encourage firms to seek technical superiorities which they are unable to exploit for their own benefit, there remains an important debate. This is between those who argue that a degree of market power and ability to earn super-normal profit encourage research, innovation and the commercial development of new technology and those who believe a high level of market competition, including price competition, forces firms to achieve maximum technical efficiency. In short, it can be argued that innovation and technical efficiency become survival conditions for competitive markets. As usual in this type of controversy there is evidence to support both views although the main weight of opinion among economists tends to be in favour of competition as a spur to technical efficiency.

Economies of Scale

It is also necessary to take into account that the monopoly firm is operating on a larger scale than the relatively small firms within the perfectly competitive market. As the size of the firm increases it should be gaining the benefits of those economies of scale that were identified in Chapter 3. This is illustrated in Fig. 11.3.

If the increase in scale of the firm's operations does lead to scale economies and the consequent reduced unit costs, then the benefits associated with the resulting saving in resources must be offset against the deadweight welfare loss. In Fig. 11.3 the short-run marginal costs of the competitive industry are represented by the curve SMC_c so that the industry produces at the output level of Q_c at a market price of P_c. If the industry suddenly becomes a monopoly and the monopolist enjoys scale economies then short-run marginal costs falls to SMC_m and the profit maximising output moves to Q_m with a market clearing price of P_m.

Looking again at Fig. 11.3, we see that a comparison between price levels P_m and P_c indicates an area of deadweight welfare loss of ABX. However, the monopolist produces at output level Q_m at a lower unit cost than could be achieved by competitive firms at that output. There is thus a saving of resource cost of P_cXGJ resulting from economies of scale that should be set against the deadweight welfare loss. In many cases we would expect the saving to outweigh the loss.

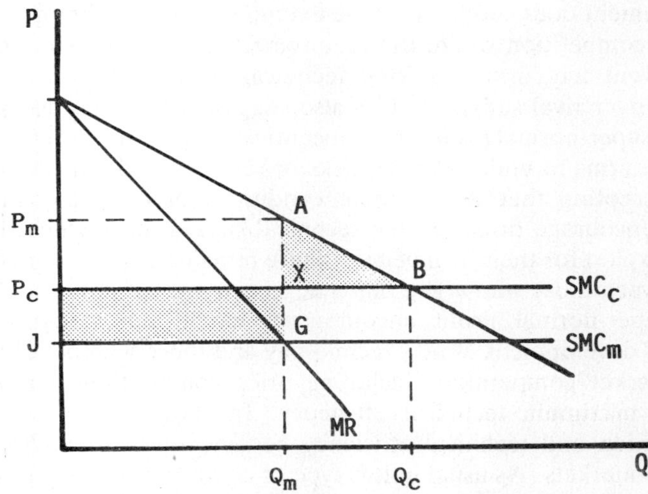

Fig. 11.3 Deadweight welfare loss and economies of scale
If the monopolist enjoys economies of scale and reduces short-run marginal costs from SMC_c to SMC_m there is a saving in resource costs of P_cXGJ which should be set off against, and may outweigh, the deadweight welfare loss of ABX.

Further Comparison of Perfect Competition and Monopoly

There are a number of further points in addition to those already made in relation to the welfare arguments surrounding perfect competition and monopoly.

Monopoly, it is argued, avoids the duplication of resources inevitable when numerous firms are competing for the same customers and offering very similar products. One of the price regulating bodies of the 1960s was critical of the apparent waste of resources involved when several bread delivery vans trundled up and down the same streets selling much the same bread. On the other hand, this criticism overlooked the element of customer service provided by competing salesmen who knew that dissatisfied customers could readily switch to a rival. Once again the debate between competition and monopoly appears inconclusive.

Even the apparently strong welfare case for achieving conditions where price equals marginal cost has its critics. There is a mathematical theory of the second best which suggests that ideal conditions cannot be achieved in all markets and it is better not to seek partial achievement. Because a modern economy will contain some monopolies, including those in the public sector, the theory casts doubt on the value of attempts to make a limited number of industries become perfectly competitive.

Imperfect Competition

Most of the analysis in this chapter has been used on comparisons of the two extreme market structures. We have earlier recognised that the majority of modern markets are likely to fall between these extremes. We have seen that monopolistic competition has many similarities to perfect competition and oligopoly tends to have many features of monopoly. If we ignore these labels we can usually say that the greater the degree of market concentration the closer firms' behaviour will come to that predicted for monopolist. Indeed, in some forms of collusion, oligopolists in a very highly concentrated market can achieve negotiated monopolies in agreed geographical regions or in the supply of specific products.

However, if economic analysis is unable to lead us to definite conclusions in the debate between perfect competition and monopoly it is unlikely to be more conclusive for imperfect competition. On the other hand, it does seem possible that some forms of imperfect competition are likely to offer the worst features of both structures. Monopolistic competition, for example, offered no significant savings in resource costs and the model introduced in Chapter 9 implied that production would be at levels above the minimum short-run cost and at a price level above that of marginal cost.

There are many uncertainties in the analysis of oligopoly but we have seen the strong incentives for collusion. We can deduce that firms are more likely to collude in the interests of their managers, shareholders and trade unions rather than to further the interests of customers.

Clearly, therefore, economic theory does not identify an ideal market structure which would be:

1 Possible to implement in either the private or public sectors of real world economies.
2 In the long-term interests of the members of the firm, i.e. shareholders, managers and workers.
3 In the long-term interests of the customers.
4 In the interests of the community which desires scarce resources to be used efficiently in both an economic and a technical sense.

In the absence of a clearly definable market structure which a government could promote as an ideal, public policy becomes uncertain and open to controversies and conflicting interests.

Welfare and Public Policy

Objectives of Public Policy

In spite of the apparent lack of firm guidelines from economic theory, governments have not been able to ignore the detrimental effects of anti-competitive business practices. It must be remembered that all government policies arise from political as well as economic motives so that the policies of particular governments depend on their political beliefs and objectives. It is possible, however, to identify a number of general principles that have frequently been important influences.

a The desire to protect individuals against powerful business interests and recognition that there is often a need to give the force of law to requirements to supply information, to make fair agreements and to protect individuals against unsafe goods and unethical practices.
b The belief that private profit is not the best or most efficient motive for providing certain goods and services for which there are individual or community needs and that some resources should be used as planned and directed by the political machinery of the State.
c A belief that individuals and the community are best served by the maximum level of competition between privately owned business enterprises operating in unregulated economic markets which, therefore, have to be protected against the monopolistic tendencies of large private or public sector organisations.

Although there may be substantial agreement over policies designed to check short-term abuses there is clearly some conflict between objectives ***b*** and ***c***, so that a government devoted to free market economics is likely to approach competition and monopoly policy from very different standpoints to one dedicated to an extension of State planning and control. Differences in fundamental political beliefs regarding the relationships between individuals and the State must be taken into account when reviewing any country's policies as they relate to business competition and market conduct.

The Development of Policy in the United Kingdom

In order to understand the present situation in the United Kingdom it is desirable to outline the main developments as they have taken place since civil servants and ministers responsible for co-ordinating the 'war effort' and organising war-time production really became aware of widespread business collusion and its implications for prices during the 1940s.

1940–1973

The first need was for reliable and unprejudiced information on the behaviour of monopolists and the extent of restrictive (anti-competitive) practices. Accordingly, a Monopolies and Restrictive Practices Commission was set up in 1948 and this produced a series of reports confirming that restrictions on competition were widespread and used both to establish and maintain the power of monopolists in many important sectors of industry. The need for government action was clear and a Restrictive Practices Court was established by the Restrictive Trade Practices Act of 1956. The Commission became the Monopolies Commission with fewer members and limited powers of investigation.

This marked a division between policies on monopolies, as such, and on certain defined restrictive trade practices. The division was one of official attitudes as well as of institutions. Government policy towards monopoly, as such, appeared to remain largely neutral and still concerned with gaining more information about specific firms and industries. On the other hand, the 1956 legislation introduced the principle that restrictive trade practice agreements made by firms collectively should be assumed to be against the public interest, with the responsibility of proving that any particular restrictive agreement might be an exception lying firmly with the parties to that agreement. In 1964 the Court's powers and a similar assumption concerning the public interest was extended to individual price fixing arrangements, which had enabled manufacturers to determine the prices and conditions under which their products could be distributed and sold to the final consumer.

In 1965 interest returned to the monopoly question against a background of a business merger movement which was significantly raising the levels of market concentration throughout most sections of industry and commerce. The Monopolies and Mergers Act (1965) gave the British Government powers to control mergers by reference to the Monopolies Commission. Many reasons have been suggested for the increase in merger activity in this period. One suggestion has been that restrictive trade practices had formerly enabled small firms to survive and limited the power of larger and more efficient firms to compete. These practices were being effectively controlled so that small firms were losing their protection and were anxious to come under the umbrella of larger organisations, while these used mergers as a method of regaining their domination over markets which they had previously manipulated through collusive trade agreements.

Another feature of the period was the growth of conglomerate mergers, combining companies of diverse interests to form large groups cutting across traditional industry boundaries. This may have been associated with the belief that the principles of business and financial management were the same regardless of the nature of productive activity and, in some cases, with the desire to seek security through diversification in a period of major economic, social and technological change when some important, long-standing industries were declining or under threat of decline. Later experience has shown that many of the conglomerates formed during this period did not achieve their declared objectives and were themselves taken over or 'unravelled' during the 1980s. The fundamental economic principle of specialisation has been reinstated and there is now a greater realisation that there are important managerial differences between, say, manufacturing and distribution or between distribution of consumer goods and the provision of financial services.

1973–1988

The Fair Trading Act of 1973 brought policies on monopolies and restrictive practices back together by setting up an Office of Fair Trading (OFT) under a Director General of Fair Trading, with general responsibilities for advising the British Government on competition and consumer protection policy. The Director General took over direct responsibility for the Restrictive Practices Court, becoming effectively the Registrar for Restrictive Trade Practices, with powers to decide which practices to challenge in the Court. He also gained powers to examine mergers and decide which should be recommended to the responsible Secretary of State for investigation by the re-named and strengthened Monopolies and Mergers Commission (MMC).

Under the 1973 Act, as under earlier legislation, the main test of perceived monopoly power was based on levels of horizontal market concentration. Firms or groups of firms operating together, which controlled at least 25% of supply in a national or regional industry, were specifically signalled out for consideration, although firms could also be considered if their merging involved assets over a stated amount. Special considerations applied to the already highly concentrated newspaper industry.

The OFT and Secretary of State gained wider powers under the Competition Act of 1980. This brought public sector organisations, such as water authorities and nationalised industries, under scrutiny. Special 'quick' references could be required from the Commission into very widely defined 'anti-competitive' practices or mergers thought likely to result in such practices. Consequently, almost any merger could be referred to the Commission under one or other of these two Acts if the Secretary of State so disposed. In fact, by 1988, successive Secretaries of State had established the view that the guiding principle for merger references should be the extent to which a proposed merger seemed likely to affect competition in the market. The Government also believed that, in most cases, competition was likely to be the best guarantee of consumer protection, but it also recognised the need for special measures to protect users of financial services so that a series of regulatory boards were set up under the Financial Services Act (1987).

Possible Policy Developments

Criticisms of British Policy on Competition

Most comment on British Competition policy starts from the belief that measures between 1948 and 1988 have been rather ineffective, since this period has seen an almost continuous increase in the level of business concentration in virtually every sector of industry and commerce. It has seen a number of periods of intense merger activity and, by 1988, almost all British companies seemed to be vulnerable to the threat of take-over.

Business criticism of British policy does not seriously challenge its ineffectiveness but does argue that it is unpredictable. Although very few mergers are seriously considered for reference to the Commission, fewer actually referred and even fewer blocked by the Secretary of State on the Commission's recommendation, the expense and trouble caused to those unfortunate enough to be selected are very considerable (around £0.5 million in at least one case) and the delay caused by reference can itself have financial and market consequences. Similar criticisms are levelled against policies on monopolies.

There is less agreement, however, with the approach that changes in policy should take. One school of thought wishes to make policies more certain, with the conditions under which mergers are permitted stated clearly by Statute, with defined mergers clearly expressed as being against the public interest, and the responsibility of proving this lying with companies which believed that their case was exceptional. In effect, policies on mergers would be modelled on existing machinery for restrictive trade practices. Supporters of this view cite American and West German policies as possible examples to be followed.

Opponents of this view argue that, in practice, neither the American nor the West German provisions have been any more successful in preserving genuine competition than British measures and that more rigid policies mainly provide new wealth creating opportunities for lawyers. Firms able to afford sufficiently clever lawyers can usually find ways round specific Statutes so that the letter of the law is preserved, but its intentions thwarted. Opponents of statutory measures believe that they would not be effective, but would add considerably to business costs and to the legal complexities of mergers.

In the light of these criticisms there are those who argue that business practices are not the proper subject for government regulation and that the regulatory and investigative machinery developed since 1948 should be swept away, thus leaving the market to decide which firms should be taken over and which should survive and grow bigger. History, however, suggests that business markets, in which governments signal their intentions not to intervene, become less competitive and more organised to benefit suppliers at substantial costs to customers.

An Appendix at the end of this chapter lists some significant MMC Reports, together with notes on the decisions the reports have contained.

The Case for and Against Mergers

The economic balance sheet in relation to mergers can be summarised in the following way:

1 The threat of take-over, which is usually detrimental to the careers and income of the senior management of the take-over victim, is a powerful spur to the efficient use of resources by existing management. It has been argued that this threat provides a significant check to the growth ambitions of management and ensures that growth rates are kept in a reasonable relationship to profit rates. Without the threat of take-over there would be no effective way of ensuring that an industry used its economic resources effectively. For example, in the 1950s and early 1960s the brewing industry failed to realise the value of scarce city sites, occupied by low profit licensed houses, until brewers started to fall victim to more alert property development companies.

2 Although some mergers undoubtedly have beneficial economic effects, the most powerful motive for merger seems to be the desire to reduce competition by eliminating competitors. This, quite clearly, leads to the less effective use of scarce economic resources and to market behaviour which favours producers at the expense of consumers. This, in fact, reverses the idea of consumer sovereignty, which has always been put forward as one of the most important benefits of the free-market economy.

Recognising that all was not well with Competition Policy, the British Government, in 1988, was undertaking a major review with the objective of introducing new legislation. In general, the Government expressed its desire to encourage competitive markets in the interests of consumers and the promotion of business enterprise. No major changes seemed to be envisaged for the general principles underlying merger policy, but the Monopolies and Mergers Commission was to be encouraged to be swifter and provision was proposed for companies to pre-notify their intentions to the Office of Fair Trading. The OFT could obtain undertakings designed to remove any potential threat to competition and obtain decisions from the Secretary of State so that companies would know at the earliest possible stage whether or not their plans were to be subject to investigation by the Commission.

The Government was planning to stiffen the law on restrictive trade practices and, in general follow the line of European Community law. It proposed to give the Office of Fair Trading greater powers to investigate suspected concealed restrictive agreements and to impose severe penalties on parties to agreements which are uncovered. However, at the time of writing proposed changes were still being discussed and you should ensure that you are fully aware of the current law relating to monopolies, mergers and restrictive trade practices. Certainly the need to ensure harmonisation between British and European law and procedures was highlighted by the temporary embarrassment suffered by the British Government when the European Commission objected to the terms of the 1988 merger between Rover group and British Aerospace.

Exercises relating to Chapter 11

1 Is competition always desirable from the point of view of consumer welfare? Support your answer with economic analysis.

2 In what ways can a government control oligopolistic power? Is it possible for governments to reduce market entry barriers?

3 The government of the USA, in contrast to most European countries, has tended to be more concerned with opposing the market power of large business groups. Discuss possible reasons for this difference in policy.

4 Discuss the view that British policies on monopolies and mergers should be modelled more closely on the official policies and practices applying to restrictive trade practices.

5 Are unregulated consumer product markets the best guarantees of consumer sovereignty and the best protection against anti-competitive business practices?

6 Choose one report of the Monopolies and Mergers Commission published since 1970. Outline the problem investigated; summarise in your own words the Commission's findings. Comment on these in the light of any subsequent developments relating to the firm(s) or industry(ies) investigated. Also note any other MMC reports whose findings may appear to agree or conflict with those in the report you have chosen.

7 Discuss the problems of defining an appropriate market for the purposes of establishing the extent of competition, bearing in mind the general relaxation of trade barriers within the European Community planned for 1992.

Appendix: The Monopolies and Mergers Commission

In 1988 the Monopolies and Mergers Commission had three main functions, which it exercised at the request of the Director General of Fair Trading and the Secretary of State for Trade and Industry, acting within powers granted by the Fair Trading Act 1973 and Competition Act 1980. These were:

1 To investigate cases of apparent uncompetitive behaviour and possible abuses of monopoly power by dominant firms within specific industries.
2 To investigate proposed mergers and take-over bids which appeared likely to result in a restriction on competition.
3 To investigate aspects of the conduct and performance of certain organisations in the public sector.

The MMC is asked to make recommendations so that any restriction of competition or abuse of monopoly power shall be removed or avoided.

Over the years the work of the Commission has been criticised, usually on one or more of the following grounds:

a Lack of analytical rigour in some of its reports.
b Lack of consistency in judgements.
c Willingness to accept high rates of profit, said to result from superior business efficiency.
d Unwillingness to consider the structure of industries and markets and willingness to confine its attention to the behaviour of firms.
e Readiness to accept assurances of changed behaviour from firms.
f Time taken over reports and expense to firms involved and the taxpayer.

Taking into account the length of time the Commission has been operating, the range of industries and firms investigated and the changing economic and market environment in which it has been operating, some of these criticisms are hardly surprising. It is fair to point out that there are also inconsistencies and disagreements among economists in their assessment of the work of the Commission and its influence on business behaviour. Most agree that it has had virtually no influence on market structure.

Comments and summaries of major reports can be found in a number of standard texts on industrial or managerial economics. The Annual Report of the Office of Fair Trading gives details of recent issues and a comprehensive Review of UK Monopolies and Mergers policy was made in Government Green Paper (A Review of Monopolies and Mergers Policy, Cmnd 7198) in 1978. At the time of writing, the most recent summary of government proposals was contained in a White Paper (DTI – the Department for Enterprise, Command 278) published in January 1988, but at this time further Green (discussion) papers were promised before new legislation, promised in the Queen's speech of 1988, was introduced.

Students are strongly recommended to look at one or two reports for themselves. These all contain convenient summaries of findings. Teachers are likely to have their own favourites but the following is a very short selection.

A Monopoly Behaviour

Year	*Firm(s) and Market*	*Issues*	*Findings and Recommendations*
1966	Kodak, colour film	Profits, marketing strategies, retail margins	Price reductions marketing changes encouragement of competition
1970	Metal Box Metal Containers	Marketing behaviour freezing out competition	End all offending practices
1973	Kelloggs Breakfast cereals	Profits, prices	Keep prices and profits under review
1976	Unilever Frozen foods	Special discount & stocking agreements with stores	End offending practices
1986	ICI and Staveley (British Salt) White salt	Lack of competition & price fixing	End price fixing, industry kept under review
1986	Foreign package holidays	Complex monopoly and preventing travel agents from discounting	End practices and allow more price competition
1987	TWIL Ltd Steel wire fencing	Market domination predatory pricing price discrimination selling restrictions	No abuse of market power but improve communications with buyers

B Mergers

Year	*Companies*	*Industry*	*MMC Findings*
1986	P & O European Ferries	Cross channel Ferries (partial merger)	Not against public interest
1987	Trusthouse Forte and Hanson Trust	Hotels, motorway and roadside catering (partial sale)	No significant reduction in competition, not against public interest
1988	Book Club Associates & Leisure Circle	Book clubs (partial sale)	Would limit competition. Allow merger subject to revision of Concordat between booksellers

C Public Sector

Year	*Bodies*	*Issues*	*Findings*
1987	British Waterways	Efficiency and costs	Managerial Deficiencies and improvements necessary
1987	Central Electricity Generating Board	Efficiency and costs	Weaknesses in marketing, financial control and general management, improvements suggested
1987	British Rail (SE Network)	Efficiency and standard of service	Service improving but not satisfactory and against public interest

12

Factor markets

Factor Markets in General

Some Features of Factor Markets

In the markets for factors of production it is the business organisations, whether of the private or the public sector of the economy which are the buyers. This has two important implications:

1 The markets tend to be more highly organised than consumer markets with a greater and often more successful attempt to grade the 'good' being offered for sale or hire. Buyers are more aware of and better informed about quality differences.
2 The demand for the factor is **derived** from the demand for the product or products which can be produced from the factor.

Questions concerning the relationship between product and factor demand are important in economics. If we take the view that firms employ factors in order to achieve profits then the quantity of any factor employed will depend on its contribution to profit. This, in turn, will depend on the relationship between the cost of employing additional factor units and the money return they contribute to the firm.

Suppose we take a very simple example based on employing varying quantities of one variable production factor, labour say, with all the others (call these capital) held constant. Suppose too that the product sells in a perfectly competitive market where the firm is able to sell all it can produce at the ruling market price. The contribution which a factor can make to the firm is then given by the marginal physical product at the various possible levels of employment multiplied by the product's price which, in this market structure, is also the firm's marginal revenue. This, therefore, is simply the change in output generated by the additonal factor multiplied by the marginal revenue of goods sold and can be called the **marginal revenue product** (MRP). An illustration is shown in Fig. 12.1a. The shape of the curve assumes that the marginal physical product of the factor exhibits diminishing returns.

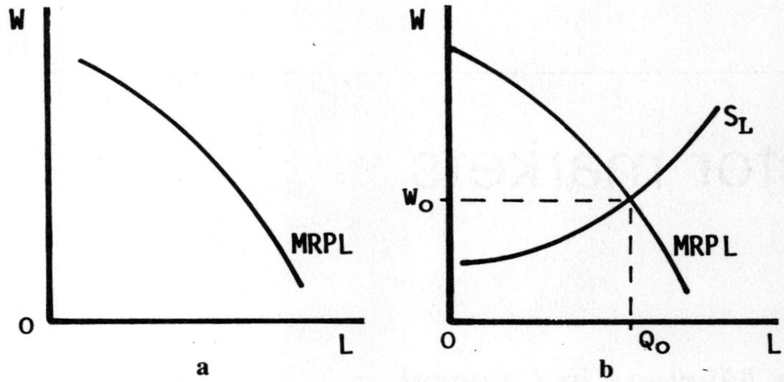

Fig. 12.1 Labour demand and supply
Fig. 12.1a shows the firm's demand for labour. Fig. 12.1b shows the firm's demand. Given supply S_L the firm's demand will be based on its own marginal revenue product for labour **MRPL** and it will require Q_0 units of labour.

So far, we have considered only the firm's demand for labour. The aggregate demand from all firms supplying a particular, competitive market will be related to the individual demand curves but will not simply be derived by aggregating these individual curves. When total product supply to the market rises, the product's market price will fall and this will be reflected in each firm's marginal revenue product. Nevertheless, the aggregate market demand is still based on the contribution made by the marginal labour units to the revenue received by all firms producing for the market.

If we abandon the idea of the perfectly competitive market for the product and assume that the firm's demand and average revenue curve is downward sloping, i.e. to sell a larger quantity of product the firm will have to reduce price, then, as explained in Chapter 7, the price is no longer the same as marginal revenue. However, the factor's contribution to the firm is still represented by its marginal revenue product which, for all profit maximising firms, will be the basis for the firm's demand for labour.

The MRP curve indicates the quantities of labour that the profit maximising firm would want to hire, assuming that capital is held constant, and that factor employment is subject to profit maximising motives only. Given these conditions, we can find the equilibrium quantity that will be employed if we know labour's supply curve. This is illustrated in Fig. 12.1b.

Economic Rent

The market price for a production factor is the result of the pressure of market forces, i.e. in an unregulated market, the interaction of market supply and market demand. The market equilibrium price is the price at which the marginal factor at quantity level Q_1 in Fig. 12.2a is just willing to enter the market. As we are here using the example of labour the market price is the market wage.

The existence of a labour supply curve implies that there are some workers, those on the curve above Q_1, who will require a wage higher than W_1 to tempt them into the market. This is presumably because they can earn more than W_1 in other markets.

On the other hand there are some workers on the curve below Q_1 who would have been willing to enter the market at a wage below W_1. Nevertheless, because the market price is W_1 this is what they receive. Wilingness to enter the market at a lower price suggests that the best available earnings in other markets is below W_1. The wage received by one of these workers, at say, Q_2, therefore, is made up of two parts. One is the minimum price necessary to tempt him into the market; this is the worker's **transfer earnings**, (W_2 in Fig. 12.2a), because it represents the best available earnings outside this market. The other is the excess over transfer earnings (W_1–W_2 in Fig. 12.2a) resulting from the need to set market price at a level high enough to attract into the market workers with higher transfer earnings. This excess is called **economic rent**. Only the earnings of the marginal worker contain zero economic rent.

If we look at the market as a whole we can again show the division between economic rent and transfer earnings. This is shown in Fig. 12.2b, where the market equilibrium wage is W_0 so that the area of economic rent is represented by W_0XM and that of transfer earnings is MXQ_0O. In an economy where social and unemployment benefits are payable it is assumed that no workers are willing to work for a wage below M. You will

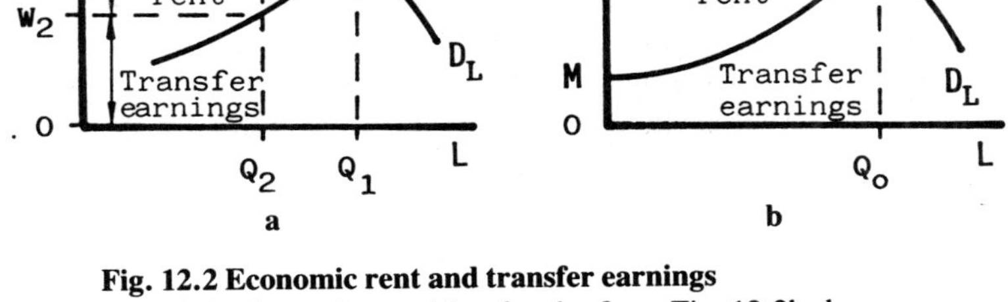

Fig. 12.2 Economic rent and transfer earnings
Fig. 12.2a shows the position for the firm. Fig. 12.2b shows economic rent and transfer earnings in the labour market.

find some computer exercises on this concept in self-assessment section eight of the disc.

The original concept was developed in terms of land at a time when the growing demand for food was bringing more and more land into cultivation. Increased food prices were making it worth while to cultivate poorer land and permitting land owners to charge higher rents for this land. At the same time, the landowners were able to obtain higher rents from land which would still have been used for food crops even if food prices and rents had been lower. The concept of economic rent showed that land rents were the result, not the cause of, the high food prices of the day.

Today, the same idea is more commonly applied to labour earnings and it helps to explain how a worker made redundant from one firm may have to accept reduced earnings before obtaining employment elsewhere. He loses the economic rent element in his pay and has to accept his transfer earnings. The concept also illustrates the vulerability of a worker who is able to exploit a monopoly talent and enjoys high earnings as long as the monopoly exists and with it a high level of demand for his services. For example, a professional footballer may enjoy a high income as long as he is scoring goals for a successful club. When his goal scoring prowess (and power to attract crowds) declines he may quickly have to revert to his transfer earnings, which, if he has no other skill, will be rather low.

Quasi-rent

Quasi-rent is the term used to describe an economic rent which arises out of a temporary market situation. Sport again provides a clear example. Suppose there is a successful television series featuring a sport which had previously enjoyed only a limited appeal. The sport suddenly gains a mass following and the relatively few existing professional players suddenly achieve super-star status and earnings. Even players of mediocre standard can enjoy high earnings for a time as they gain employment as coaches or give local exhibitions. However, the high earnings attract other sports people. Talented amateurs find it worthwhile to develop their skills professionally and standards start to rise. After a time, only a relatively few very gifted players are able to enjoy high incomes. Below them, large numbers of hopefuls struggle to make a living. All but the most gifted revert to their transfer earnings or remain in the market at the lower end of the supply curve. At this stage, the quasi-rent no longer exists and just a very few achieve genuine economic rent from their monopoly supply of a very high level of skill.

The Labour Market

Imperfections of Labour Markets

Economists are interested in the national or macromarket for labour, particularly in the national imbalance between supply and demand which can lead to large scale unemployment. This macroeconomic problem, however, is outside the scope of this chapter which is more concerned with individual markets for particular industries, occupations or skills, i.e. the micreconomic aspects of labour markets.

Most markets for labour are highly imperfect. Almost none of the conditions necessary for perfectly competitive markets are likely to be found in a labour market. The good 'labour', is rarely homogeneous. Attempts are often made to grade some labour skills. Typists, for example, may be paid according to the typing speeds they are able to achieve but few employers would regard one typist as being exactly like another. People vary enormously in the quality of the work they do and the interest they show in their work.

Communications in labour markets are often poor. People may be unaware of job opportunities in their own firms and those with jobs do not constantly look for other jobs in other firms. Transport and other costs usually mean that the worker's net wage actually available for spending is very different from the gross wage paid by the employer.

Market power is commonly found on both the supply and the demand side of markets. The Government, in one form or another is either the sole, or by far the largest, employer of many workers, including teachers, electricity supply workers and coal miners. There are relatively few banks and insurance companies so that some grades of financial workers may be effectively prevented from changing employment beyond a certain age and grade. On the other hand, trade unions and professional associations may be able to control entry to certain occupations very effectively, through examinations, apprenticeships or simply through the rigid application of 'closed shop agreements' with employers. In some cases these agreements ensure that recruitment is controlled by a single union. Movement from one occupation to another, or even movement between firms in the same occupation, can be very difficult and sometimes not possible above a certain age.

People do not work purely for economic motives. There are strong social pressures which determine that people are expected to work and social considerations influence the type of work that people choose or prefer to do. An occupation, such as publishing, may be fashionable even though wage rates may be generally lower than in less socially attractive industrial occupations. Some people may value leisure or the ability to control their work more highly than pay. Many self-employed people achieve for themselves an hourly rate that would be completely unacceptable if offered to an employee.

There is also a time element in labour rewards that is difficult to incorporate into the simple analysis of wage rates. Both employer and employee may regard a work contract as an investment from which each expects to receive future benefits in return for present sacrifice. A worker may accept what he considers to be low pay in the early years of employment in return for training with a reputable firm that will improve his future market price. An employer may pay a young 'trainee' more than the value of his current marginal product in the hope that this will improve in the future. When economic conditions make it possible, some employers will be willing to pay some older workers a wage in excess of current marginal productivity in recognition of past services. The more highly skilled the worker and the more personal his or her contribution to production the greater the chance that time will be a factor influencing the wage paid.

Wage Differentials

Wage rates and wage earnings differ because there are very many different micromarkets for labour each with differing conditions of supply and demand. It is, however, possible to identify some major influences that tend to produce differing wage rates:

1 **Education** In general, work that requires a relatively high standard of education tends to be better paid than work without this requirement. As a consequence, it is again generally true that earning capacity increases in proportion to the length of time spent in full-time education. This does not, of course, mean that every person who remains in full time education to gain a PhD is guaranteed the highest possible income. The link between education and pay is just a general tendency from which there are very many individual exceptions.
2 **Skill** Among manual workers, the higher the level of skill the higher generally is the average pay.
3 **Sex** Although there has been equal pay legislation for some years the average earnings of female workers tends to be between two-thirds and three-quarters of equivalent male workers. There are several reasons for this. More women than men work part-time. Women tend to break off careers to devote themselves to families just at the age when men are looking for promotion and increased pay. Socially, women are still expected to put home and family before career and this means that women tend to follow husbands's careers more frequently than the reverse and employer expectations of female priorities may influence their judgement when recruiting and making promotion decisions.

4 **Geography** There are still regional differentials in the pay of people in similar occupations although these are not as great as in the past. There are also differences in regional living costs, particularly the costs of housing and travelling to work so that the net and gross regional wage tables may look very different. Gross pay is highest in London and the South East but these are also the areas of highest housing and travel cost. A bank employee who can walk to work from a leafy suburb in a small provincial town may enjoy a style of living far superior to that of his commuting London colleague whose gross salary may be much higher. The tendency for large national employers and trade unions to produce national wage scales and to reduce regional differentials may actually have had the effect of increasing the real net disparities in earnings and living standards.

5 **Industry** We must not forget that ultimately the demand for labour is derived from the demand for the product of labour. The more value placed by the community on the product, the higher the value of the marginal physical product of labour and this will be reflected in the firm's marginal revenue product of labour. If an industry is prospering then wages of all forms of labour employed in that industry are likely to be higher than those of equivalent workers in declining industries.

6 **Trade Unions** The ability of workers to organise themselves to control the conditions of recruitment and working relationships with employers can influence wage rates. It is, nevertheless, easy to over-emphasise the effect of union power. Students often quote the example of mineworkers who improved their relative pay in the 1970s, apparently by militant action. They tend to forget that the massive oil price rises from 1973 onwards raised the value of coal and hence the marginal product of coal workers. Their pay might have increased even more rapidly under conditions closer to perfect competition. Because the question of trade union influence on wages is such an important one this aspect is examined further in the next section.

You may have noticed that the above influences indicate that wages tend to be higher when demand is relatively high and consistent and when supply is likely to be inelastic and restricted, whether by the natural shortages of rare human qualities or by artificial restrictions imposed by trade unions or professional associations. In practice, while demand and supply are important for wage determination, wages are more than just the price of labour. More advanced and detailed studies indicate that there are many social and economic forces operating on wage differentials some of which have a very long history and are not explicable entirely in terms of modern labour markets. You should be aware that this chapter provides only an introduction to a very large area of study.

Determinants of Trade Union Influence

It is usually believed that trade unions will most easily be able to raise members' wages without sacrificing their jobs when:

1 The demand for labour is wage inelastic.
2 The costs and difficulties of organisation are low.

The following conditions are likely to make labour wages inelastic:

a A low degree of price elasticity for the product of labour
b Few technical possibilities for substitution between labour and capital or other production factors
c Lack of available supply of substitute factors
d When labour costs are a relatively small proportion of total costs

It is largely on these grounds that the success of some skilled unions in keeping their members at or near the top of the wages league has been explained. Changes in technology, however, can reduce the barriers to entry to product markets and so reduce the power of a skilled union. Printers have been discovering this fact following the introduction of modern electronics to printing.

The costs of union organisation are more likely to be low when the following conditions apply to the workforce:

a Stability and continuity of work so that workers are not subject to large scale lay-offs and do not change jobs frequently
b Heavy concentration of workers in a relatively few firms and work establishments
c A high level of concentration of workers in a few production locations or geographical areas
d A high degree of loyalty to trade union principles and practices and readiness to identify with union objectives. Some areas and industries have very long and strong trade union traditions.

Another approach to the same question is to use normal economic analysis to show the effects of changes in market structure. When, for example, employers are selling their output under conditions approximating to perfect competition, normal supply and demand analysis suggests that a union will have difficulty in raising wages above the labour market equilibrium rate without sacrificing the jobs of some members. On the other hand, a powerful union facing an employer who is a monopolist in the product market and perhaps a monopoly buyer (monopsony) of a particular category of worker, may be able to raise pay without sacrificing jobs and may even increase both wages and employment. What the union is doing is to appropriate some of the employer's monopoly profit to the benefit of its members.

Clearly, there are many issues relating to this aspect of factor pricing but at this stage of study we can only indicate general areas and suggest that you pursue some of these more closely. You can also test your understanding of these arguments by working through the computer exercises in section eight of the self-assessment disc.

The Capital Market

The Demand for Capital

The demand for business capital, in the sense of productive machines and equipment, is derived from the demand for the product of capital. At this stage we shall assume that a firm is most likely to want additional capital if it believes that it can profitably expand its production capabilities. For the firm, the investment decision, i.e. the decision whether or not to make use of money capital in order to acquire new physical assets, is concerned with comparing the cost of the capital required for the acquisition with the increased future profit that can be anticipated as a result of acquiring the assets.

It does not matter whether the firm already has the money capital in reserve or whether it must borrow it or raise it by some form of share issue. However it is acquired, money capital always has an opportunity cost. In the case of money already in the firm's own bank accounts, there is the opportunity cost measured in terms of the next best investment opportunity outside the business.

Introduction to Investment Appraisal

If we assume that the cost of a proposed investment project is known, e.g. a specialised piece of machinery costing £100.000, the problem is to find out how much additional profit is likely to be earned by the firm in the future as a result of acquiring the machine and then to relate this to the cost. The additional future profit resulting from an investment is likely to be in the form of a flow of funds received at intervals in the future. Suppose we can estimate this flow with a reasonable degree of certainty. Suppose the anticipated flow is in the following form:

Additional profit flow (revenue – cost in each year) resulting from investment in a new machine costing £100 000

At the end of Year 1	£25 000
At the end of Year 2	£40 000
At the end of Year 3	£40 000
At the end of Year 4	£45 000

The total flow of additional profit is £150 000. Can we then say that at the end of four years the investment will show a gain of £50 000?

Even if we are completely sure that the projected gains will, in fact, be achieved there are two further points that we need to take into account:

1 £100 received today is not the same as £100 received in a year's time. Money can earn interest. If I have to wait for a year before being paid, I lose the interest that the payment could have earned if invested, say, in a bank deposit account. The longer I wait, the more interest I lose and the less is the present equivalent of that future payment.

2 When considering the value of one possible project we must take into account other available possibilities. We have to ask what is being sacrificed if we decide to spend the £100 000 on the machine. What, in fact, is the **opportunity cost** of the money employed in the investment project?

Point **1** warns us that we should take into account the earnings ability of money when calculating the value of any flow of future payments or profits. We should, therefore, **discount** the future payments in order to bring them to their equivalent **present value** (PV). The present value of a payment due in the future is, then, that amount which, if invested at a rate of return equivalent to the chosen discount rate will produce an amount equivalent to the future payment.

Point **2** shows us that the discount rate used as a basis for appraisal should be based on the cost to the firm of the capital it employs.

Assuming that we have been able to estimate the flow of revenues (R) and costs (C) likely to be generated by an investment project and the appropriate discount rate or rates (d) during the period of the project's life, we can calculate the PV of the flow of net revenues. Then, deducting the original cost incurred at the start of the project we have the **net present value (NPV)**.

$$NPV = (R_0 - C_0) + \frac{(R_1 - C_1)}{(1 + d)} + \frac{(R_2 - C_2)}{(1 + d)^2} + \ldots + \frac{(R_n - C_n)}{(1 + d)^n}$$

where

$(R_0 - C_0)$ relates to the net revenue at the start of the project's life
$(R_1 - C_1)$ and $(R_2 - C_2)$ . . . $(R_n - C_n)$ relate to the first and subsequent years
d represents the chosen discount rate, expressed as a decimal fraction, e.g. 15% = 0.15

We can now take another look at the earlier set of returns resulting from the expenditure of £100 000. If we take a discount rate for the period of 10% we can produce the following table:

Year	*£000 (R – C)*		*Discount factor*		*£000 PV*
0	−100				
1	25	×	$\frac{1}{(1.1)}$	=	22.727
2	40	×	$\frac{1}{(1.1)^2}$	=	33.058
3	40	×	$\frac{1}{(1.1)^3}$	=	30.053
4	45	×	$\frac{1}{(1.1)^4}$	=	30.736
			Total PV	=	116.574
			NPV (PV – C_0)	=	16.574

Finding present values is made less tedious by the use of discount tables. Suppose we raise the discount rate to 16% and use tables to find the appropriate discount factor (present value of £1 payable in n years). We can now present the table in the following form:

Year	*£000 (R – C)*		*Discount factor*		*£000 PV*
0	−100				
1	25	×	0.862	=	21.55
2	40	×	0.743	=	29.72
3	40	×	0.641	=	25.64
4	45	×	0.552	=	24.84
	NPV (total PV – C_0)			=	1.75

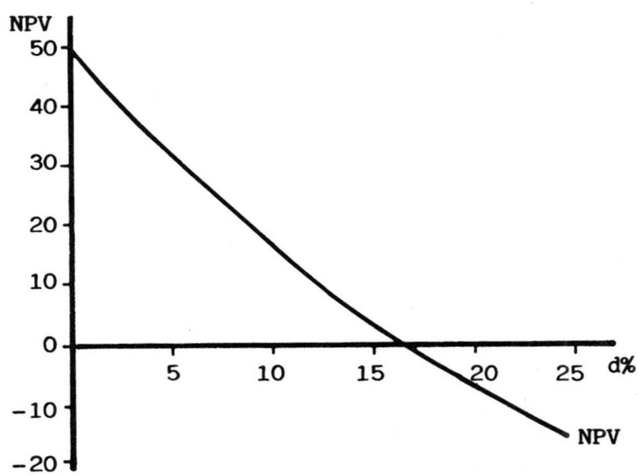

Fig. 12.3 Net present value and internal rate of return
The curve shows **NVP** at discount rates from 0% to 25%. The **IRR** where **NVP** = 0 is 16.8%.

At this higher discount rate, the NPV has fallen to £1750. Notice how the PV falls as the discount rate rises. This, of course, is what we would expect. The higher the opportunity cost of money the greater must be the future payment to compensate for this sacrificed earning power.

This relationship can be illustrated in the form of a graph. Fig. 12.3 is based on our example. It shows that the NPV falls to zero at a rate of 16.8%. Now the rate of discount which brings the PV of a flow of future payments to equality with the initial cost of an investment, i.e. which produces an NPV of zero is called the **internal rate of return** (IRR).

Firms which base their investment decisions on IRR have a target cost of capital which proposed investments must achieve to be considered as practical proposals.

We can now summarise the methods of appraising proposed investment projects using NPV or IRR:

1 *If the firm can obtain a limitless supply of capital:*
- ***a*** Any project with an NPV>0 should be undertaken
- ***b*** Any project with an IRR greater than the firm's target cost of capital should be undertaken, provided that this target does truly relate to a realistic opportunity cost of capital

2 *If there is a limited supply of capital to the firm:*
- ***a*** Projects with the largest NPV should be chosen
- ***b*** Projects with the largest IRR should be chosen

This simple introduction to the very large and important subject of investment appraisal cannot include a serious discussion of the problems actually encountered in the choice of discount rates, nor in the estimation of future profits. Even at this stage, however, you should be able to appreciate that when discount rates are very high, PVs are very low and only the most profitable projects with high returns early in their lives are likely to be considered. You should also realise that uncertainty about future demand, future interest rates or government economic measures will further complicate the work of appraising projects and further reduce the number likely to be acceptable. Uncertainty is always seen as the enemy of business investment.

Payback Period

Firms frequently apply a very simple first test of a project to find out if further investigation and calculation are likely to be worth while. This involves working out the length of time which must pass before the total net revenues (not discounted) equal the initial or total cost of the project. This is called the **payback period**. Only those projects which fall within the firm's minimum acceptable period are allowed further consideration. This method is not suitable on its own as a final test because it is not based on discounted values and it ignores the money flows anticipated beyond the payback period.

In addition to a number of relevant self-assessment questions in section eight, there is also an investment appraisal programme included as section seven of the simulations in the computer disc. This programme enables you to experiment with projects of your own and calculates payback periods, NPVs and IRRs from figures supplied by you. From this programme you can readily see the effect of differing discount rates and project life periods. With its help you can gain some interesting insights into many aspects of investment appraisal.

In this chapter we have been looking at some important features of the demand for business capital. Further aspects of the demand for money and of finance markets as they affect the economy as a whole are normally studied within the field of macroeconomics.

Exercises Relating to Chapter 12

1 Why are labour markets, viewed as economic factor markets, normally imperfect?
2 Why do accountants usually earn more than their secretaries?
3 How do trade unions seek to raise the pay of their members?
4 Should trade unions oppose productivity pay bargaining?
5 Use the investment appraisal programme on disc 2 to answer the following questions which relate to projects A and B below:

A		B	
Year	**Revenue**	**Year**	**Revenue**
0	−10000	0	−10000
1	6000	1	1000
2	4000	2	2000
3	2000	3	2000
4	1000	4	4000
5	1000	5	7000

a Assuming that an investment decision to choose either A or B is to be based on NPV alone, which project will be chosen at a discount rate of: *i* 6%; *ii* 12%?
b Using one diagram draw the graphs of the NPVs of both A and B at discount rates between 0% and 15%.
c At what discount rate (other things being equal) would a decision based on NPV be indifferent between projects A and B?
d If a firm had sufficient finance to invest in both projects what would be the maximum discount rates at which A and B would be worthwhile?
e Which project would be chosen on the basis of payback period only?
f If an investment decision based on IRR appears to suggest a different result from one based on NPV, does this mean that these methods are unreliable guides for investment managers? Justify your answer.

6 Discuss the effects on business investment of:
 a a prolonged period of high inflation in which product prices and factor costs are rising.
 b a period when general political and economic conditions are uncertain.

13

Some practical aspects of economics

Economics and Reality

Most of the topics we have considered in this book may appear to bear very little relation to the 'real' world. You have probably heard or perhaps made the comment that, 'this is all right in theory but of no use in practice.' You have also probably heard the jibe about asking six economists for their advice and receiving twelve opinions. A former President of the USA was reputed to have commented, 'Oh for a one handed economist!'

Such comments as these raise the whole question of how economists develop and test their theories. What is the normal **methodology** of economics.

The Deductive Approach to Analysis

In common with most other scientists, economists usually employ a form of scientific methodology which is termed **deductive reasoning**. This involves taking a number of logical steps:

Step 1 Identify the problem or phenomenon which it is hoped to explain.

Step 2 Identify those variables which are thought likely to influence the problem. These might be the result of theoretical analysis, hunch or earlier research.

Step 3 Select those variables which are considered to be the most influential or important. This deliberate simplification implies the rejection of some of the finer points of detail. How far to take the simplifying process is a matter of judgement. If we reject too much we depart too far from reality; if not enough we retain so many 'realistic' variables that satisfactory analysis becomes impossible.

Step 4 Combine in a logical manner the assumptions that have been retained to form a **model** or theory.

Step 5 Use the model to generate some predictions. For example, we can have a model of an economic market which predicts that changing one variable, say price, influences another, say quantity sold. These predictions can be generated either through oral reasoning or, more usually today, through mathematical modelling.

Step 6 Collect data on the variables included in the model.

Step 7 Compare the model's predictions with actual experience. That is to say the model is **tested**. If the two conform we say that the theory on which the model is based has been **verified**. This does not necessarily mean that it is true, but simply that it is supported by the evidence of the limited amount of data used in the comparison. If, however, the model's predictions differ from the data then we say that the theory has been **refuted**. Refutation would mean a return to Step 2 and a fresh start.

From time to time, economists may be faced with a number of models and theories which appear to explain the same evidence equally well. When this happens they tend to select whichever model uses the least number of assumptions. In this way the models are honed down (using Occam's razor) until they contain the minimum of necessary assumptions.

This is a logical process and can lead to the development of some powerful theories but it can also mean that these can be accused of being unrealistic. The refining of models over time combined with the simplifying of assumptions of Step 2, always exposes the economist to the charges described at the beginning of this chapter. It is always difficult to have a cake and eat it at the same time!

This brings us to the further controversy of how to test the models. Should we test the assumptions or just the predictions? Once again, there is no easy solution to this problem and the only honest answer is to say that it depends on the original objectives.

If we are solely interested in predictions then we do not need to worry too much about the assumptions as long as the predictions are accurate. If, on the other hand, we wish to influence the performance of a part of the economy, it is important to understand the mechanism whereby the predictions are generated. For this we need realistic assumptions. Professor Friedman has pointed out that it is possible to make fairly accurate predictions concerning the performance of a billiard player on the assumption that he had a good working knowledge of the laws of motion. As long as he played well it would not matter whether he had this knowledge or played by instinct. If he started to play badly, however, it would probably help to arrange for him to attend some seminars on the laws of motion.

Positive and Normative Approaches

The last methodological issue which we ought to consider is the difference between **positive** and **normative** economics.

The models examined in this book are mainly positive in that they examine the consequences of changing one or more variables in a model. The same conclusions could be reached by anyone starting with the same assumptions. They are the result of a series of logical deductions. When the consequences of a change have been predicted it is possible to argue over whether they are good or bad. This question of good and bad takes us into the field of welfare or normative economics which is concerned with what **should be**. Positive economics is concerned with what **is** regardless of its desirability.

The following illustration should clarify the difference between positive and normative. Certain landowners in eighteenth century England found that they were losing game birds and animals from their estates. Analysis of the problem suggested that the game was being poached illegally by local men. The landowners sought a solution through the setting of mantraps which trapped and broke the leg of anyone unfortunate enough to step on them. Subsequent generations have banned the use of such defences on the grounds that physical cruelty to a human being is a greater crime than theft. This introduction of a moral consideration or a **value judgement** brings us into the normative field. Normative economics is concerned with what is desirable for the welfare of the community. If we ignored all normative aspects of the mantrap solution to poaching we would be concerned only with its effectiveness and with the relative costs of the losses compared with those of using the traps.

This somewhat extreme example also helps to explain why six economists may have more than six opinions. The same problem can be viewed from several different viewpoints. Different assumptions may be made and different interpretations are possible from the same facts. Finally, the predictions can be judged from the standpoint of different value judgements.

This, of course is only a very brief introduction to the major methodological problems associated with economics but it should help you to understand some of the current controversies more fully. It is against this background that we now examine how the regression option may be used to test a simple model based on the analysis developed in Chapter 6.

The Demand for Cars

Our objective is to explain the changes that have occurred in the total number of new cars registered in the UK between 1967 and 1978. In the light of Chapter 6 we would expect the quantity demanded of cars to be influenced by a range of variables such as price, the prices of other goods, income, advertising, running costs, insurance, petrol prices and so on. Clearly, the number of variables is too great too handle in a simple model so we need to identify those we consider to be the most important. At this stage we adopt the hypothesis that the most important are **price** and **income** so that our model becomes:

Q = f(price, income)

If we now set out to test the statistical strength of these relationships we have to recognise that many variables have been neglected and that these will affect the quantity of sales. To take account of this we include, in our model, an error term 'e' which is designed to embrace all the neglected variables. The model thus becomes:

Q = f(P,Y,e)

where:

Q = number of cars registered
P = prices of cars
Y = disposable income levels
e = the error term

If we have correctly identifed the most significant variables there is a high probability that, over a period of time, the error terms will have a **mean** of 0. (The mean is a simple arithmetic average, as in a player's average score in cricket, which is the total runs scored by the player divided by the number of innings in which he has played.) If it does, this will suggest that the variations attributable to the neglected variables are small and cancel each other out.

In order to test the model we have to make the relationship between the variables explicit. If, for simplicity, we assume that the relationship is linear (can be expressed in the form of a straight line) then this can be expressed in the form of:

$$Qd = a + bY + cP + e$$

where:

Qd = the number of new car registrations
Y,P and e = the same as before
a = the level of registrations which would occur even if income and price were zero
b = the strength of the relationship between registrations and income (Y)
c = the strength of the relationship between registrations and car prices

This means that a one unit change in income will lead to a $1 \times b$ unit change in registrations and a one unit change in price will lead to a $1 \times c$ unit change in registrations.

To test your understanding of the demand influences can you say what signs (+ or −) the values of b and c should have? Are b and c the same as the income and price elasticities of demand?

Having formulated the model we wish to test, the next step is to collect data on the three variables concerned. The data we have used in this example came from the following sources:

1 The quarterly new car registrations were obtained from the annual reports of the Society of Motor Manufacturers and Traders.
2 The income figures were obtained from the journal, **Economic Trends**, and represent disposable income (income after tax and certain compulsory deductions) adjusted for inflation to represent income at constant (1970) prices.
3 The price series had to be specially constructed to take into account the differences in car models and in the prices, less trade and other discounts, actually paid by customers.

In constructing the price index, basic model prices were taken from **Autocar**. Adjustments were then made to take into account differing market shares of the models and for changes in general price levels over the period. The necessity for constructing a special series of car prices illustrates a common problem faced by economists, i.e. that all the information they need is unlikely to be found readily at hand in the form required. Obtaining basic information is often a major part of any attempt to test a theory.

The sets of data of 50 quarters were then fed into the regression programme of disc 2. The programme identifies the values for a, b and c which minimise the sum of all the squared errors. These values form the so-called least squares line. It is necessary to square the errors to eliminate the difference between errors which are above(+) and below(−)the line. Squaring a negative number, of course, makes it positive and capable of being handled with the positive numbers squared.

The following example illustrates this principle. It uses a two-variable model so that we draw a normal two-dimensional graph. In this model, sales (Y) are considered to be a function of (directly dependent on) income (X) only. The relationship can be expressed in the form:

$$\hat{Y} = a + bX$$

Plotting sales against the vertical axis and income levels against the horizontal axis, we can mark actual sales levels for corresponding income levels with an x. This produces a scatter of crosses as shown in Fig. 13.1a. The least squares program of disc 2 will generate a straight line conforming to the equation $Y = a + bX$ and this is illustrated in Fig. 13.1b.

Observing one quarter denoted by p, the actual level of sales is Y_p

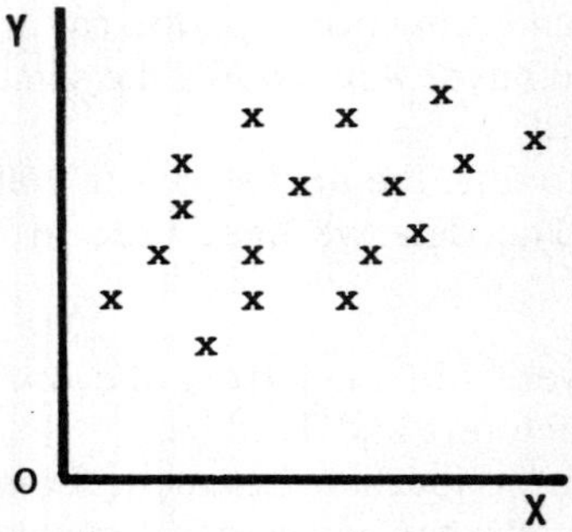

Fig. 13.1a A scatter diagram

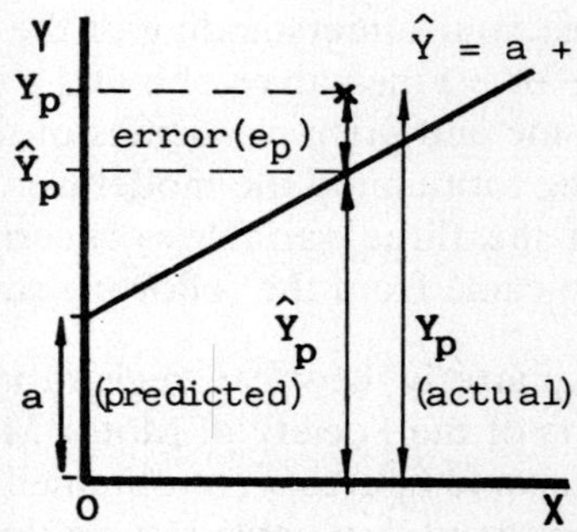

Fig. 13.1b The least squares regression line

whereas the sales predicted by the model would have been at the level $\hat{Y}_p$. The symbol ˆ (hat) is usually used to signify a predicted figure. The difference between the two figures is the error for that quarter, expressed as $e_p = Y_p - \hat{Y}_p$. The least squares straight line selects those values of a and b which minimise the sum of these errors squared.

For the technique to have any real statistical meaning, the error term must have certain properties, one of which is that its arithmetic mean must equal zero. A discussion of the other properties is beyond the scope of this book but can be found in any good statistics textbook.

The following results were generated from actual data by the regression program:

	Mean	*Standard deviation*
Y	313.53	65.388
X1	8915.74	994.867
X2	111.13	37.326

Correlation Coefficients

	Y	*X1*	*X2*
Y	1	0.485	0.246
X1	0.485	1	0.83
X2	0.246	0.83	1

Regression line

$$Y = -117.112 + 0.59X1 - 0.88X2$$

t values (−1.231) (4.166) (−2.32)

$$R^2 = 0.314$$

where

Y = new car registrations in thousands
X1 = real disposable income adjusted to constant (1970) prices
X2 = new car prices adjusted to constant (1970) prices

The figures show that, on average, for the 50 quarters which had been examined the number of cars sold was 313 530. The **standard deviation** provides us with some information concerning the spread of the data around the mean – it is a form of average of the deviations of the figures from the mean using a similar squaring technique to combine positive and negative signs as that explained earlier. The larger the standard deviation (**sd**) the more widely spread are the figures around the mean. A figure of 65 388 tells us that for approximately two thirds of the time, the new registrations fell within + or −65 388 of the mean sales of 313 530.

The correlation matrix provides an indication of the degree of association between pairs of the variables. Two features should be noted, the sign (+ or −) and the size of its square. A positive sign (+) suggests that the two variables increase or decrease together but a negative sign (−) suggests that an increase or decrease in one is associated with the reverse movement in the other. The square of the correlation coefficient indicates the percentage of the deviations in one variable that can be 'explained' by changes in the other.

The correlation coefficient between Y and X1 is +0.485 indicating that as income increases so do new registrations. The correlation coefficient squared $(0.485)^2 = 0.235$. This suggests that 23.5% of the changes in registrations can be explained by changes in income, or that 23.5% of the changes in income can be explained by changes in registrations. We have to remember that the coefficient says nothing about causation. Indeed there may be no direct relationship between two variables with a high correlation coefficient. For instance, it is claimed that there is a good correlation between the number of storks flying over Lowestoft and the number of babies born each year!

The regression equation tells us that if income and price were zero, − 117 112 registrations would be made! These sales would, in practice, be generated by factors unaffected by income and price but which would remain at a constant level. The income coefficient of +0.057 suggests that each income increase of £1m will be accompanied by a rise in new registrations of 59. The positive sign suggests that motorcars are a normal good as defined and explained in Chapter 6. Fortunately for normal demand theory, or for our calculations and programme, the negative sign (−0.88X2) indicates that an increase in the price index is accompanied by a fall in new car registrations. It suggests that a 1% change in the index will be associated with a decrease in sales of 880. If the signs or the size of the coefficients were substantially different from those expected, the validity of the model would come into question.

Having considered the economic significance of the coefficients, we must examine the statistical significance of the error term. We need to know whether the size of the price coefficient (−0.88) is due to the influence of price on registrations or whether it could be attributed to a random figure generated by the error term, i.e. attributable to demand influences which we decided not to investigate.

Here the t values printed in brackets below the coefficients go some way to resolving this problem. If the coefficients were caused by the random influences only, we would expect what is known as the standard error (the unexplained fluctuations likely to arise in any set of statistical data) of the coefficient to lie within a certain range of the mean value. The coefficient, therefore, is divided by its standard error and the result is compared with a number which would be generated if it were the consequences of random influences only. The coefficient divided by its standard error is called the **t value**. The actual t value should be compared with the standard t value for 50 observations to be found in any set of statistical tables. A reasonable rule of thumb is that for more than 30 observations, the appropriate t value is approximately 2. Below 30 observations the value rises and above it gets smaller, tending towards 1.96.

In our example, the t value for income (X1) is 4.166. This is greater than 2 so we may deduce that the coefficient of 0.059 is greater than would be expected from a random variation and income changes are associated with new car registrations. If we accept the assumption that changes in income cause changes in the demand for cars then we may say, with a 95% degree of confidence, that income is a significant determinant of new car registrations. An explanation of this 95% level of confidence or significance can be found in any good statistics textbook. For the purposes of this example, we can simply point out that 100% certainty is impossible in this life and we often have to work within acceptable degrees of probability. If, however, the t value had been less than 2 then the coefficient generated would not have been large enough for us to be confident that it had not been caused by a purely random variation. We would have to conclude that the true coefficient was zero and that the variable did not explain any of the changes we have been investigating. This, in fact, is the case with our constant.

Finally, the regression coefficient (R^2) tells us the proportion of changes in registrations (Y) that can be explained by price (X2), income (X1) and the constant (a). This, of course, implies acceptance of the assumptions underlying the model, i.e. that prices and incomes are determinants of the demand for cars. In our example, the equation explains only 31.4% of the new car registrations over the 50 observations. This is not really very impressive and not sufficient to claim that our model has been verified. This program has provided figures to suggest that both price and income are statistically significant influences on new car registrations but only explain 31.4% of the changes. On the basis of this result, we would have to reject our simple model and develop another to include one or more additional variables.

This type of result is not unusual when looking at demand relationships.

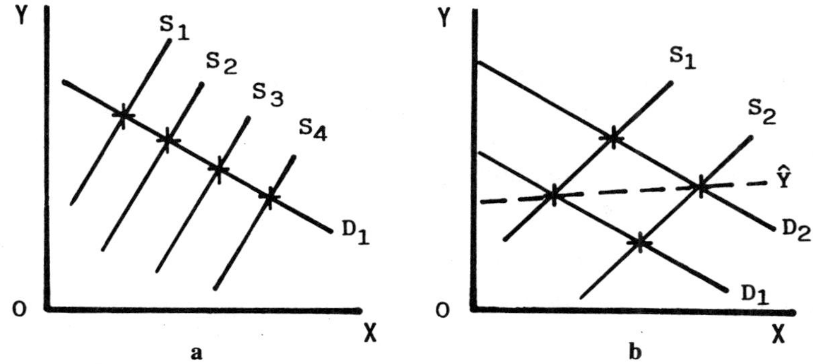

Fig. 13.2 Stable and unstable relationships over time
Fig. 13.2a shows a stable demand relationship. Only the supply curve moves and the demand curve is easily identified. Fig. 13.2b indicates that both demand and supply have changed and the regression line ($\hat{Y} = a + bX$) reflects neither the demand nor the supply relationships.

They occur because price is the result of both demand and supply forces and we have been examining one side of the relationship only. The identification problem that can arise is illustrated in Figs. 13.2a and 13.2b which show 4 possible observations relating price and sales.

In theory, we would hope that the demand relationship had stayed stable in each of the 4 years in which observations are recorded so that these reflect only the movement of the supply curve. This is shown diagramatically in Fig. 13.2a. Unfortunately both relationships often change over time. This is suggested by Fig. 13.2b. As a consequence of these concurrent changes, the regression line which is produced is not a full reflection of either a demand or a supply relationship.

This problem, the so called identification problem, can be extremely difficult to overcome and is beyond the scope of this book. Nevertheless, it should be recognised by anyone using the regression package.

Conclusion

These thirteen chapters have provided the core of what is generally accepted as the theory of microeconomics. At the same time, we have shown how much of the theory can be applied to the real world and have concluded with an example illustrating some of the methods and difficulties faced when economic analysis is applied to actual conditions.

The computer exercises and simulations contained in the discs provide ample opportunities for you to test your understanding of the analytical concepts and methods introduced in the book. The investment appraisal and regression programmes provide additional facilities for you to experiment with your own figures and for you to practise analysing data available in the many statistical sources which are now available.

We believe that intelligent use of the discs and textbook can give you an understanding of the value and limitations of economics in a way that is not possible with standard text and workbooks.

Exercises Relating to Chapter 13

No detailed exercises are given for this chapter because groups will be constrained by the sources available to them. We do suggest that UK students should become familiar with the **Business Monitor** series of industrial statistics and seek sales data from firms and the main trade associations.

Index